SSAT Elementary Level Practice Tests

SSAT Elementary Level Practice Tests

Three Full-Length Verbal and Quantitative Mock Tests with Detailed Answer Explanations

Anthem Press
An imprint of Wimbledon Publishing Company
www.anthempress.com

This edition first published in UK and USA 2024
by ANTHEM PRESS
75–76 Blackfriars Road, London SE1 8HA, UK
or PO Box 9779, London SW19 7ZG, UK
and
244 Madison Ave #116, New York, NY 10016, USA

British Library Cataloguing-in-Publication Data
A catalogue record for this book is available from the British Library.

Library of Congress Control Number: 2023947233
A catalog record for this book has been requested.

ISBN-13: 9781839990915 (Pbk)
ISBN-10: 1839990910 (Pbk)

This title is also available as an e-book.

Contents

Introduction

About SSAT

The Secondary School Admission Test (SSAT) is a standardized test used by admission officers to assess the abilities of students seeking to enroll in an independent school. The SSAT measures the basic verbal, math, and reading skills students need for successful performance in independent schools. Every year, 80,000+ students take the SSAT to apply to independent schools. There are two types of SSAT administrations.

Grade Level

Students of grades 3–11 can register for one of the three SSAT tests, depending on their grades:

- The Elementary Level test is for students currently in grades 3 and 4.
- The Middle Level test is for students currently in grades 5–7.
- The Upper Level test is for students currently in grades 8–11.

The SSAT Elementary Level has four sections (in order of testing): Quantitative Math, Verbal Reasoning, Reading Comprehension, and a Writing Sample which is written by the students in response to a given writing prompt. Each section is designed to tap into a unique aspect of a student's preparation for academic work.

How does a student arrange to take the SSAT?

Students may take the SSAT in one of the following ways:

1. **Paper SSAT:** This is the most popular and preferred option. Parents can register for paper-based test by creating an account on https://portal.ssat.org/SAP/Tests/NewRegistration.
2. **Flex Testing:** This increases the availability of the paper SSAT beyond the standard testing dates. Consider Flex testing when the standard dates or locations don't work for your schedule. There are two types of Flex testing:
   - Open Flex tests—are when a school hosts a group of students for Flex testing and makes registration open to the public.
   - Closed Flex tests—are when an educational consultant or school administers the SSAT to an individual or a small group of students.
3. **At-Home Testing:** The SSAT at Home is a computer-based version of the SSAT taken on designated testing dates at pre-scheduled times.
4. **The Prometric SSAT:** This is a secure, computer-based version of the SSAT taken at Prometric test centers. It is the same reliable test as the paper and SSAT at Home versions. Note that SSAT Elementary Level is not offered by Prometric.

What types of questions are on the SSAT?

The first three sections are composed of multiple-choice questions. In the fourth section, the Writing Sample requires the student to respond to a preselected writing prompt.

The first two sections, Quantitative Math and Verbal Reasoning, measure the applicant's reasoning ability.

The Verbal Reasoning test consists of two types of items: vocabulary and sentence completion.

At the Elementary Level, the Quantitative Math test conforms to national mathematics standards and ask the student to identify the problem and find a solution to it. The items require one or more steps in calculating the answer.

The next section, Reading Comprehension, the student is asked to read a passage and then answer items specific to that passage.

The Essay is written by the student in response to a writing "prompt" or topic that is grade-level appropriate. The prompts rotate throughout the testing season. They are designed to prompt a student to write an informed essay on a particular topic.

The table below gives a quick snapshot of the questions in the SSAT:

Test Section	Questions	Time	Details
Quantitative (Math)	30 Questions	30 minutes	Multiple-choice questions composed of math computation based on grade-level math topics.
Verbal Reasoning	30 Questions	20 minutes	Vocabulary and analogy questions.
Reading Comprehension	28 Questions	30 minutes	Reading passages with multiple-choice questions based on reading the passages.
Writing Sample	1 Question	15 minutes	The writing sample is not scored, but schools use it to assess writing skills.

What is the format of the test? All questions are multiple choice

What is the medium of the test? Computer based

How to use the book

- Before you start the test, read the directions for each section and note the time allocated.
- Ensure that you have a continuous block of time available to complete the entire test—including all the sections.
- When you take the practice test, remove all possible distractions including your phone.
- Take the entire test in one sitting—this is very critical to get a realistic view of how you would do in the real test.
- Check your answers right after the test.
- Review the explanations on the same day, so you remember why you chose a particular answer.
- Before starting the next practice test, review the answers that you got wrong from the previous test and the explanations so you don't make the same mistakes.

SSAT Results

Use these attached sample reports to familiarize yourself with the SSAT score reports. You'll also find detailed explanations of each section below. There are two types of scores:

SSAT Scaled Scores: Each of the three main Elementary Level test sections is scored on a scale of 300 to 600, with a total scaled score range of 900 to 1800. Each of the three main Middle Level test sections is scored on a scale of 440 to 710, with a total scaled score range of 1320 to 2130. Each of the three main Upper-Level test sections is scored on a scale of 500 to 800, with a total scaled score range of 1500 to 2400.

SSAT Percentiles: SSAT percentile rankings range between 1% and 99% and show how a student performed as compared to other students in the same grade and of the same gender who have taken the SSAT during the past three years.

Learn more about SSAT scoring here: https://www.ssat.org/about/scoring/ssat-score-report

SSAT Elementary Level Exam 1

The
SSAT
+ Elementary

SECTION 1

QUANTITATIVE MATH

Time—30 minutes
30 Questions

Following each problem in this section, there are five suggested answers. Select the best answer from the five choices.

Example

Answer: (A) ● (B) (C) (D) (E)

5,413 – 4,827 =

(A) 586
(B) 596
(C) 696
(D) 1,586
(E) 1,686

The correct answer to this question is lettered A, so space A is marked.

1. If 7 is added to a number, the answer is 26. If the same number is added to 12, what is the sum?

(A) 31 (B) 37 (C) 19 (D) 29 (E) 27

2. Simplify the given expression:

$$\frac{4}{9}+\frac{2}{3}+\frac{1}{18}$$

(A) $\frac{6}{7}$ (B) $\frac{10}{9}$ (C) $\frac{6}{18}$ (D) $\frac{7}{6}$ (E) $\frac{9}{10}$

3. If all sides are equal, what is the perimeter of the given figure below?

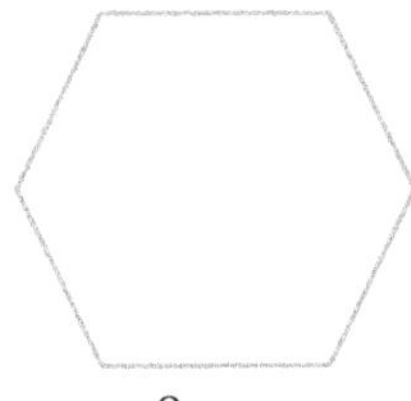

8 cm

(A) 42 cm (B) 56 cm (C) 48 cm (D) 54 cm (E) 52 cm

4. Find the missing value of the sequence: 3, 5, 8, 13, 21, ____, 55, 89.

(A) 30 (B) 34 (C) 36 (D) 32 (E) 28

5. Chloe is making strawberry jam. She needs 15 strawberries to make 1 bottle of the jam. If she wants to make 3 bottles of strawberry jam, how many strawberries does she need?

(A) 30 (B) 48 (C) 40 (D) 45 (E) 42

6. Round up 94,478 to the nearest tens.

(A) 94,400 (B) 94,480 (C) 94,470 (D) 95,480 (E) 94,500

7. Which is greater than $\frac{7}{9}$?

(A) 0.43 (B) 0.57 (C) 0.70 (D) 0.65 (E) 0.80

For questions 8 and 9, refer to graph below:

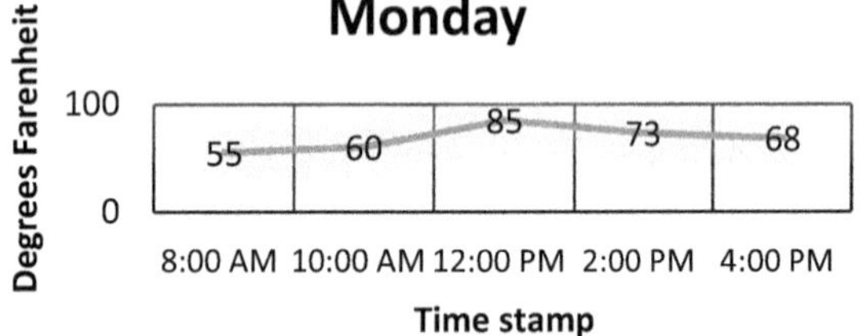

8. What was the recorded highest temperature?

(A) 85°F (B) 60°F (C) 73°F (D) 68°F (E) 55°F

9. What time did the highest temperature occur?

(A) 8:00 pm (B) 10:00 pm (C) 12:00 pm (D) 2:00 pm (E) 4:00 pm

10. If $154 + 297 - x = 37$, what is the value of x?

(A) 400 (B) 404 (C) 414 (D) 424 (E) 410

11. What is 130% of 40?

(A) 55 (B) 40 (C) 42 (D) 50 (E) 52

12. Matt's friends are planning to throw a birthday party for him. They will be equally splitting the expenses. If they collected $50, how much did each of them contribute?

(A) $10 (B) $12.50 (C) $7.25 (D) $5 (E) cannot be determined

13. In the given figure, the shaded circles are what fractional part of the whole set of circles?

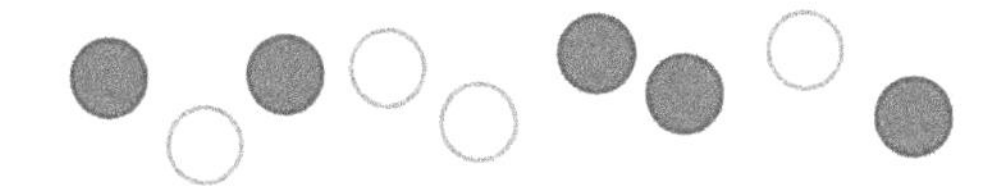

(A) $\frac{1}{9}$ (B) $\frac{5}{9}$ (C) $\frac{4}{9}$ (D) $\frac{2}{9}$ (E) $\frac{2}{3}$

14. If $4(a - b) = 28$ and $a = 3$, then what is the value of b?

(A) 7 (B) – 3 (C) 3 (D) – 4 (E) 5

15. In the triangle below, what is the value of x?

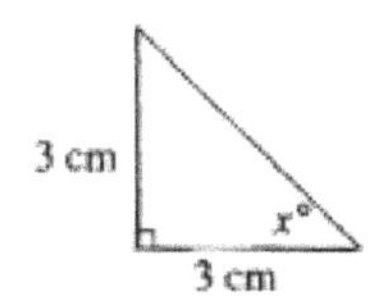

(A) 60° (B) 20° (C) 45° (D) 30° (E) cannot be determined

16. In the Venn diagram below, the shaded region shows those people who bought what fruit?

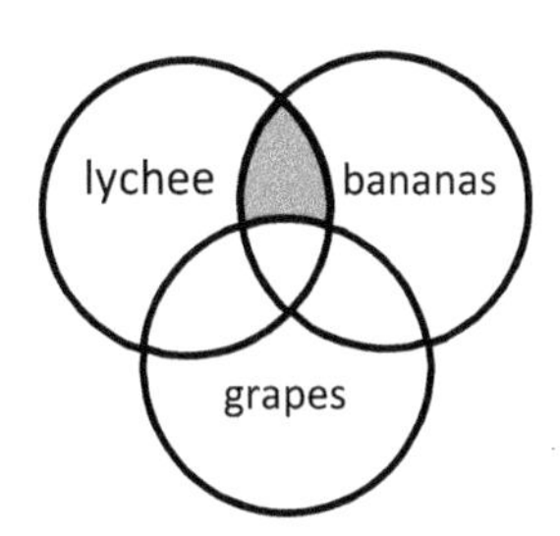

(A) bananas and lychee (B) grapes and lychee (C) grapes and bananas

(D) lychee and grapes (E) bananas and grapes

17. A popular rural area has four villages. The populations of these villages are 571, 1249, 801, 645. Which of the following shows the populations in order of largest to smallest?

(A) 1249, 645, 801, 571 (B) 1249, 801, 571, 645 (C) 1249, 801, 645, 571

(D) 1249, 645, 571, 801 (E) 1249, 571, 801, 645

18. Mrs. Hernandez is 4 times older than her 9-year-old son. How old is Mrs. Hernandez?

(A) 42 years old (B) 36 years old (C) 45 years old (D) 40 years old (E) 39 years old

19. Marissa has a rectangular pool that is 15 ft long and 7 ft wide. Her neighbor, Josie, wants to build a congruent pool. What will be Josie's pool measurements?

(A) 7 ft long and 15 ft wide (B) 7 ft long and 14 ft wide (C) 14 ft long and 7 ft wide

(D) 15 ft long and 7 ft wide (E) cannot be determined

20. Andrew received \$10 as his pocket money for their school trip. He spent \$1.78 for his snacks, \$3.45 for the souvenirs. How much does Andrew have left?

(A) \$4.77 (B) \$5.23 (C) \$4.50 (D) \$5.50 (E) he spent all his money

21. In a jar, there are equal numbers of white, black, and pink marbles. Which of the following could be the total number of marbles in the jar?

(A) 58 (B) 35 (C) 72 (D) 47 (E) 17

22. If the shaded section of the circle in figure below signifies 46 types of flowers, then how many flowers could the unshaded section represent?

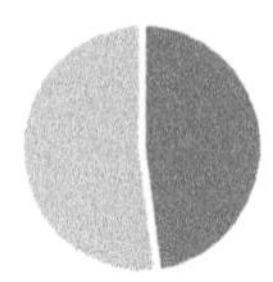

(A) 30 (B) 45 (C) 40 (D) 35 (E) 50

23. If $x + 4 = 7$ and $3y = 15$, then what is the value $y - x$?

(A) 3 (B) 2 (C) 5 (D) 4 (E) 6

24. What is the average of the following numbers? 3, 8, 11, 5, 18

(A) 8.8 (B) 9 (C) 9.2 (D) 8.6 (E) 9.6

25. Lara brought a box full of butterfly origamis. There are 12 blue, 8 red, and 10 green butterflies inside. If John wants to pick one butterfly, then what is the probability that he will pick a green one?

(A) $\frac{17}{20}$ (B) $\frac{4}{15}$ (C) $\frac{2}{29}$ (D) $\frac{3}{25}$ (E) $\frac{1}{3}$

26. Chad studied for 2 hours and 30 minutes in preparation for his math test. He started at 3:00 pm, at what time did he finished studying?

(A) 3:30 pm (B) 5:00 pm (C) 5:30 pm (D) 6:00 pm (E) 4:30 pm

27. What is the equivalent of 55%?

(A) $\frac{11}{20}$ (B) $\frac{5}{10}$ (C) $\frac{11}{50}$ (D) $\frac{22}{25}$ (E) $\frac{1}{5}$

For questions 28–30, please refer to the given situation:

Mrs. Smith conducted a survey of eye color in a class of 30 students. This is the result of the survey.

Eye Color	Number of Students
Blue	9
Brown	10
Gray	2
Green	7
Amber	2

28. What is the common eye color?

(A) blue (B) brown (C) gray (D) green (E) amber

29. What is the percentage of the students with blue eyes?

(A) 10% (B) 25% (C) 18% (D) 30% (E) 20%

30. How many students have gray and amber eye color?

(A) 4 (B) 9 (C) 10 (D) 7 (E) 1

SECTION 2

VERBAL REASONING

Time—20 minutes
30 Questions

This section consists of two different types of questions. There are directions for each type.
Each of the following questions consists of one word followed by four words or phrases. You have to select a word or phrase whose meaning is closest to the word in capital letters.

Example

SWIFT: (A) clean (B) fancy (C) fast (D) quiet

Answer
Ⓐ Ⓑ ● Ⓓ

1. ABANDON

(A) leave (B) retain (C) stay (D) withhold

2. ACKNOWLEDGE

(A) deny (B) admit (C) refuse (D) reject

3. ADMIRE

(A) hate (B) despise (C) appreciate (D) dislike

4. AIMLESS

(A) regular (B) orderly (C) organized (D) random

5. ALARMED

(A) frightened (B) unafraid (C) daring (D) fearless

6. ASSURED

(A) uncertain (B) confident (C) doubtful (D) unsure

7. ASTONISH

(A) scare (B) betray (C) absent (D) amaze

8. BIASED

(A) neutral (B) impartial (C) unfair (D) fair

9. BRITTLE

(A) elastic (B) crumbly (C) flexible (D) strong

10. CAUTIOUS

(A) careless (B) reckless (C) unwary (D) careful

11. DECLINE

(A) refuse (B) accept (C) approve (D) tolerate

12. DEFICIENT

(A) perfect (B) complete (C) incomplete (D) intact

13. ELONGATE

(A) shorten (B) cut (C) lengthen (D) reduce

14. ENVY

(A) sympathy (B) jealousy (C) kindness (D) goodwill

15. EVACUATE

(A) vacate (B) stay (C) fill (D) load

The following questions ask you to find the relationships between words. For each question, select the choice that best completes the meaning of the sentence.

Example	Answer
Ann carried the box carefully so that she would not ____ the pretty glasses.	● (B) (C) (D)
(A) break (B) fix (C) open (D) stop	

16. Ice to cold as fire is to

(A) hot (B) red (C) flame (D) matchsticks

17. Father is to mother as brother is to

(A) older (B) tall (C) sister (D) athletic

18. Large is to small as wide is to

(A) area (B) vast (C) narrow (D) far

19. Class is to students as concert is to

(A) expensive (B) fun (C) crowded (D) fans

20. Uppercase is to lowercase as bold is to

(A) prominent (B) subtle (C) font (D) striking

21. Vacuum cleaner is to dust as washing machine is to

(A) appliance (B) home (C) load (D) laundry

22. Talented as to skillful as smart is to

(A) intelligent (B) dull (C) child (D) study

23. Cotton is to soft as rock is to

(A) soil (B) hard (C) ground (D) round

24. Elephant is to mammal as snake is to

(A) venom (B) reptile (C) slither (D) long

25. Branch is to tree as petal is to

(A) flower (B) wedding (C) butterfly (D) pink

26. Gate is to metal as table is to

(A) sturdy (B) chair (C) wood (D) dining room

27. Glass is to drinking as pencil is to

(A) paper (B) lead (C) eraser (D) writing

28. Spoon is to fork as pencil is to

(A) wood (B) eraser (C) writing (D) school

29. Film is to director as lecture is to

(A) teacher (B) boring (C) learn (D) students

30. Fish is to school as lion is to

(A) pride (B) jungle (C) wild (D) ferocious

SECTION 3

READING COMPREHENSION

Time—30 minutes
28 Questions

Read each passage carefully and answer the questions about it. For each question, decide on the basis of the passage which one of the choices best answers the questions.

"You ain't goin' off on no 'possum-huntin,' Andrew," cried a sharp voice from the kitchen, where Mrs. Pearson was frying turn-over pies for dinner. "I ain't goin' to have you comin' back here with your arms shot off, or maybe your head, even. You can just <u>makeup your mind</u> to leave that gun be. You ain't goin' traipsin' around the farm with a parcel o' niggers this day; that you ain't!"

"Oh, mother, don't say that!" said Andrew. "I shoot any time with father, and I'm not the least afraid of the gun."

"Which ain't any sign it won't go off and land you where you'll be mighty willin' to own your mammy knows some things."

Mrs. Pearson was one of those women who <u>boast</u> it was, that, having spoken her mind, she never changed it. Andrew knew it was useless to argue the matter. He did attempt a little boasting, but it was very promptly <u>nipped in the bud</u>.

From A Boy's Battle *by Will Allen Dromgoole*

1. What did Andrew want to do which was declined by his mother?

(A) Andrew wanted to go hunting

(B) Andrew wanted to eat dinner at his uncle's place, but his mother was already making turn-over pies for dinner

(C) Andrew wanted to go with his father

(D) Andrew wanted to skip school

2. Why did Mrs. Pearson forbid Andrew to go?

(A) fear of accident (B) because they did not have the money to spend

(C) because there will be no adults to supervise him (D) because it was dinnertime

3. The attitude of Mrs. Pearson toward Andrew going hunting was

(A) jubilant (B) worried (C) proud (D) relaxed

4. What does "make up your mind" in the passage mean?

(A) go against (B) heed to someone's advice (C) make a decision (D) think of someone

5. What was Andrew's attitude toward his mother's refusal to go hunting?

(A) grateful that his mother was worried about him

(B) happy that his mother allowed him to do what he wanted

(C) nonchalant that his mother did not care

(D) pushy and tried arguing so he can go although his mother already said no

6. What does "nipped in the bud" in the passage mean?

(A) cut the buds before flowers blossom (B) say yes without hearing the entire message

(C) allow without questions (D) stop immediately

7. Which word is mostly like "boast"?

(A) diminish (B) minimize (C) brag (D) belittle

Astronomers have discovered twelve more moons orbiting Jupiter. The planet's moon count now stands at 92. That's the most in our solar system.

The new moons were spotted using telescopes. It took scientists about a year to confirm the discovery. The moons are small, no bigger than two miles across. Jupiter has many small moons. They could be pieces of bigger moons that crashed into other space objects.

"I hope we can image one of these outer moons close-up," says Scott Sheppard, of the discovery team. He works for the Carnegie Institution for Science, in Washington, D.C. Sheppard wants "to better <u>determine</u> [the moons'] origins." He thinks that more of them have yet to be found.

From Jupiter's New Moons *by Cristina Fernandez, Time for Kids*

8. What is the main intent of the article?

(A) to share the news about Neptune's new moons

(B) to share the news about Jupiter's new moons

(C) to report that twelve new planets have been discovered in the solar system

(D) to share the news that Jupiter has a total of twelve known moons

9. How many moons does Jupiter have after the recent discovery?

(A) 92 (B) 12 (C) 9 (D) 100

10. According to the article, have all of Jupiter's moons been discovered after the recent discovery?

(A) yes, Jupiter has ninety-two moons in total

(B) no, Jupiter has six more moons that are under the discovery team's radar and yet to be confirmed

(C) no, more the of the moons have yet to be found and is not known how many more according to Scott Sheppard, of the discovery team

(D) not implied in the article

11. What equipment did the scientists use when they discovered the new moons?

(A) microscope (B) magnifying glass (C) digital camera (D) telescope

12. How big were the new moons scientists have discovered?

(A) twice the size of Earth's moon (B) no bigger than two miles across

(C) one-fourth of the size of Jupiter (D) same size as Pluto

13. What does the word "determine" mean in the article?

(A) to come to a judgment after consideration

(B) to avoid giving a definite answer or position

(C) to get or keep away from (as a responsibility) through cleverness or trickery

(D) to get free from a dangerous or confining situation

14. Who are astronomers?

(A) a person who is skilled in the study of objects and matter outside the Earth's atmosphere and of their physical and chemical properties

(B) a person who is skilled in the science of measuring time

(C) a person who is skilled in the science that deals with the history of the Earth and its life, especially as recorded in rocks

(D) a person who is skilled in the science of marine resources and technology

The hole in Earth's ozone layer is on track to heal. That's according to a new United Nations (U.N.) report. The recovery comes 35 years after an international agreement. That deal stopped the use of ozone-destroying chemicals.

Ozone is a gas in the environment. It shields the planet against harmful radiation from the sun. This radiation is linked to skin cancer. It's also linked to crop damage.

Chemicals in refrigerants and sprays ate away at the ozone layer. Once, many products sold in stores contained these chemicals. A global agreement from 1987 led to a ban on them.

"There has been a sea change in the way our society deals with ozone-depleting substances," David W. Fahey says. He's a scientist who led the U.N. report.

With current policies, ozone covering most of the planet could fully recover by 2040. It will take until 2066 to fix the hole above Antarctica, the report says.

From Ozone Recovery *by Brian S. McGrath, Time for Kids*

15. What is the main intent of the article?

(A) to share the good news to people that ozone-depleting chemicals are now banned to help the ozone layer recover

(B) to share the devastating news that the ozone layer continues to deplete as the days go by

(C) to share the good news that the hole in Earth's ozone layer is on track to heal

(D) to invite people to stop using refrigerators at home

16. Why is the ozone layer important?

(A) it protects us from asteroids getting inside the Earth's atmosphere

(B) it shields Earth from harmful radiation from the sun

(C) it keeps our seasons on schedule (D) it helps avoid tropical cyclones

17. What agreement was made that helped in the recovery of the ozone layer?

(A) ban cigarette smoking (B) stop the production of cars

(C) prohibit fumigation (D) ban ozone-depleting chemicals in refrigerants and sprays

18. As mentioned in the article, is it possible for the ozone layer to fully recover?

(A) no, there is no hope in recovering the ozone layer

(B) no, the damage is permanent and will only get worse in time

(C) yes, with current policies, it is expected for the ozone covering most of the planet could fully recover by 2040

(D) time can only tell

19. What does the word "depleting" mean in the article?

(A) something added (as by growth)

(B) to make smaller in amount, volume, or extent

(C) to make greater in size, amount, or number

(D) to become greater in extent, volume, amount, or number

20. According to the article, how can we achieve full recovery of most of the ozone layer?

(A) evacuating the part of the Earth where the hole in the ozone is the largest

(B) turning off electrical appliances regularly

(C) continuing the current policies on the ban of use of ozone-destroying chemicals

(D) move people temporarily to a host planet

21. Which part of the ozone layer will take the longest to fix?

(A) Pacific (B) Antarctica (C) Atlantic (D) Greenland

On January 17, archaeologists in Norway said they had found the world's oldest rune stone. The flat rock is etched with runes. These are letters from an ancient Scandinavian language. They could have been carved 2,000 years ago.

"This may be one of the first attempts to use runes in Norway and Scandinavia on stone," Kristel Zilmer says. She's a professor at the University of Oslo, in Norway.

The stone has markings on it. Not all of them make sense. Some of the letters spell Idiberug. That could be the name of a person or a family.

Zilmer calls the discovery "the most sensational thing that I, as an academic, have had." The rune stone will be on show for a month. It will be at the Museum of Cultural History, in Oslo.

From A Message From the Past *by Cristina Fernandez, Time for Kids*

22. What is the intent of the article?

(A) to share the discovery of the world's oldest rune found by archaeologists in Norway

(B) to disprove that the oldest rune stone is in Northern America

(C) to teach readers how to read ancient Scandinavian writing

(D) to introduce the inventor of the ancient Scandinavian language

23. How old was the etching on the runes?

(A) 17 (B) 200 (C) 2,000 years (D) 16 BC

24. What was the writing on the rune stone about?

(A) not all the writing has been translated but some of the letters spell Idiberug which could be a name

(B) it was a detailed narrative of Idiberug's hunting day

(C) it was a list of the family members' names

(D) none of the writings were translated

25. Where will the rune stone be on display?

(A) the Museum of Cultural History, in Oslo (B) the cave where the rune stone was found

(C) the White house (D) NASA

26. Which of the words below is a synonym of "etched"?

(A) erased (B) engraved (C) made (D) shaped

27. Based on the pronoun used for Kristel Zilmer, we can assume that her gender is

(A) a child (B) a male (C) a female (D) unknown

28. What does the phrase "the most sensational thing" mean?

(A) not arousing interested or curiosity

(B) causing weariness, restlessness, or lack of interest

(C) lacking in gaiety, movement, or animation

(D) so remarkable that it causes great excitement and interest

SECTION 4

WRITING SAMPLE

Time—15 minutes

Directions:

Write an essay on the following prompt on the paper provided. Your essay should not exceed two pages and must be written in ink. Erasing is not allowed.

Look at the picture and write a story about what happened. Be sure your story includes a beginning, middle, and conclusion.

Answer Key

Section 1

1. A	6. D	11. E	16. A	21. C	26. C
2. D	7. E	12. E	17. C	22. E	27. A
3. C	8. A	13. B	18. B	23. B	28. B
4. B	9. C	14. D	19. D	24. B	29. D
5. D	10. C	15. C	20. A	25. E	30. A

1. Answer: **A**

Let x be the number. $x + 7 = 26 \Rightarrow x = 19$. The number is 19. If you add 12, then the sum will be 31, hence the answer is A.

2. Answer: **D**

To add fractions with different denominators, we need to find first the least common multiple (LCM) of the denominators. The denominators in the given expressions are 9, 3 and 18 and the LCM is 18. Next, rewrite the fractions so they share the same denominators: $\frac{8}{18}+\frac{12}{18}+\frac{1}{18}=\frac{21}{18}$. The sum is $\frac{21}{18}$ or $\frac{7}{6}$, hence the answer is D.

3. Answer: **C**

The given figure is a hexagon and to get the perimeter, use the formula $P = 6a$. $P = 6\ (8) = 48$. The perimeter is 48 cm, hence the answer is C.

4. Answer: **B**

To get the value of the next number, you just need to add the two numbers preceding that number.

In preceding numbers before the missing value is 13 and 21. Add: $13 + 21 = 34$. The missing number is 34, hence the answer is B.

5. Answer: **D**

To make one bottle of jam, Chloe needs 15 strawberries. To get the total number of strawberries needed to make three bottles of jam, simply multiply 15 with 3. $15 \times 3 = 45$. Chloe needs 45 strawberries, hence the answer is D.

6. Answer: **B**

   In rounding off numbers, if the digit in ones place is equal to or more than 5, then make the number zero and increase the digits in tens place by 1. In the given, the ones place is 8, which greater than 5, so we need to replace the ones place with zero and add 1 to the tens place, which will make it to 80. Copy the preceding number and we will have 94,480, hence the answer is B.

7. Answer: **E**

   The decimal value of $\frac{7}{9}$ is 0.77778, and among the given choices, option E is greater than 0.77778, hence the answer is E.

8. Answer: **A**

   The highest recorded temperature is 85°F, hence the answer is A.

9. Answer: **C**

   The highest recorded temperature is 85°F and it occurred at 12:00 pm, hence the answer is C.

10. Answer: **C**

    Simplify $154 + 297 - x = 37 \Rightarrow 451 - x = 37 \Rightarrow x = 414$. The value of x is 414, hence the answer is C.

11. Answer: **E**

    Multiply $\frac{130}{100} \times 40 = 52$. The answer is E.

12. Answer: **E**

    In the given situation, it did not specify how many friends Matt has, hence the answer is E.

13. Answer: **B**

    There are a total of 9 circles in the given set. There are 5 shaded circles out of 9. If we make it into fraction, we will get $\frac{5}{9}$, hence the answer is B.

14. Answer: **D**

    Substitute the value of a to get the value of b. $4(3 - b) = 28 \Rightarrow 12 - 4b = 28 \Rightarrow -4b = 16 \Rightarrow b = -4$. The value of b is -4, hence the answer is D.

15. Answer: **C**

    It is given that the sum of the interior angles of a triangle is 180°. The sides that measure 3 cm are perpendicular to each other and form a right angle. A right-angle measures 90°. It is also given that the angles opposite of the sides that are equal (pertaining to the non-hypotenuse sides) are also equal, hence the answer is 45°, which is C.

16. Answer: **A**

    The shaded part shows the intersection of lychee and bananas categories, hence the answer is A.

17. Answer: **C**

    If you will rearrange the order from largest to smallest, then you will get 1249, 801, 645, 571, hence the answer is C.

18. Answer: **B**

    Multiply 4 with her son's age to get Mrs. Hernandez's age. $9 \times 4 = 36$. Mrs. Hernandez is 36 years old, hence the is answer is B.

19. Answer: **D**

    The definition of "congruent" in geometry is identical, so Josie's pool will have the same measurements with Marissa's pool, hence the answer is D.

20. Answer: **A**

    Add first his total expenses: $1.78 + $3.45 = $5.23, then subtract it from $10: $10 – $5.23 = $4.77. The remaining amount is $4.77, hence the answer is A.

21. Answer: **C**

    There are three kinds of marbles that are equal in numbers, so the total number of marbles should be divisible by 3. Among the choices, only option C is divisible by 3, hence the answer is C.

22. Answer: **E**

    The unshaded area has more flowers than the shaded area. Among the choices, only option E is greater than 46, hence the answer is E.

23. Answer: **B**

    The value of x and y to get $y - x$: $x + 4 = 7 \Rightarrow x = 3$; $3y = 15 \Rightarrow y = 5$. Substitute: $y - x = 5 - 3 = 2$, hence the answer is B.

24. Answer: **B**

    To get the average, add all the numbers of the given set and divide the sum with the total numbers from that set. $\frac{3+8+11+5+18}{5} = \frac{45}{5} = 9$. The average is 9, hence the answer is B.

25. Answer: **E**

    There's a total of 30 butterfly origamis. The probability of getting a green butterfly is 10 out of 30 or $\frac{10}{30} = \frac{1}{3}$, hence the answer is E.

26. Answer: **C**

Two hours and 30 minutes after 3:00 pm will be 5:30 pm, hence the answer is C.

27. Answer: **A**

The fraction equivalent to 55% is $\frac{55}{100} = \frac{11}{20}$, hence the answer is A.

28. Answer: **B**

The eye color that has highest number is brown, hence the answer is B.

29. Answer: **D**

The total number of students is 30 and there are nine students that have blue eyes: $\frac{9}{30} = 0.3 = 30\%$. A total of 30% of the students have blue eyes, hence the answer is D.

30. Answer: **A**

There are two students with gray eyes and two students with amber eyes. Simply add and you will get 4, hence the answer is A.

Section 2

1. A	11. A	21. D
2. B	12. C	22. A
3. C	13. C	23. B
4. D	14. B	24. B
5. A	15. A	25. A
6. B	16. A	26. C
7. D	17. C	27. D
8. C	18. C	28. B
9. B	19. D	29. A
10. D	20. B	30. A

1. The correct answer is (A). To abandon is to leave (a place or vehicle) empty or uninhabited, without intending to return. Synonyms are to leave and forsake.

2. The correct answer is (B). To acknowledge is to accept or admit the existence or truth of. Synonyms are to admit, confess, and concede.

3. The correct answer is (C). To admire is to regard (an object, quality, or person) with respect or warm approval. Synonyms are to respect, appreciate, and regard.

4. The correct answer is (D). Aimless means without purpose or direction. Synonyms are random, scattered, and erratic.

5. The correct answer is (A). Alarmed means frightened or concerned that one may be in danger or that something undesirable will happen.

6. The correct answer is (B). Assured means sure that something is certain or true. Synonyms are confident, sure, and certain.

7. The correct answer is (D). To astonish means to make a strong impression on (someone) with something unexpected. Synonyms are to amaze, surprise, and stun.

8. The correct answer is (C). Biased means inclined to favor one side over another. Synonyms are partial, unfair, and one-sided.

9. The correct answer is (B). Brittle means having a texture that readily breaks into little pieces under pressure. Synonyms are crisp, crumbly, and fragile.

10. The correct answer is (D). Cautious means having or showing a close attentiveness to avoiding danger or trouble. Synonyms are careful, wary, and alert.

11. The correct answer is (A). To decline means to show unwillingness to accept, do, engage in, or agree to. Synonyms are to refuse, reject, and ignore.

12. The correct answer is (C). Deficient means lacking some necessary part. Synonyms are incomplete, flawed, and partial.

13. The correct answer is (C). To elongate means to make longer.

14. The correct answer is (B). Envy means a painful awareness of another's possessions or advantages and a desire to have them too.

15. The correct answer is (A). To evacuate means to remove the contents of. Synonyms are to empty, clear, and vacate.

16. The correct answer is (A). The first word pair has item and temperature relationship.

17. The correct answer is (C). The first word pair has a male–female relationship. In siblings, the counterpart is brother as the male sibling and sister as the female sibling.

18. The correct answer is (C). The first word pair is antonyms.

19. The correct answer is (D). Students attend classes while fans go to concerts.

20. The correct answer is (B). The first word pair is antonyms.

21. The correct answer is (D). A vacuum cleaner is used to clean dusts while a washing machine is used to wash laundry.

22. The correct answer is (A). The first word pair is synonyms.

23. The correct answer is (B). The first word pair has item–characteristic relationship. A cotton is soft while a rock is hard.

24. The correct answer is (B). The first word pair has animal–category relationship. An elephant is a mammal while a snake is a reptile.

25. The correct answer is (A). The first word pair has part–whole relationship. A branch is a part of a tree while a petal is a part of a flower.

26. The correct answer is (C). The first word pair has item–characteristic relationship. A gate is made of metal while a table is made of wood.

27. The correct answer is (D). The first word pair has item–purpose relationship. A glass is used for dinking while a pen is used for writing.

28. The correct answer is (B). Spoon and fork are usually used as a pair like a pencil and an eraser.

29. The correct answer is (A). The first word pair has product–producer relationship. A film is directed by a director while a teacher runs a lecture.

30. The correct answer is (A). A group of fishes is called a school while a group of lions is called a pride.

Section 3

1. A	11. D	21. B
2. A	12. B	22. A
3. B	13. A	23. C
4. C	14. A	24. D
5. D	15. C	25. A
6. D	16. B	26. B
7. C	17. D	27. C
8. B	18. C	28. D
9. A	19. B	
10. C	20. C	

1. The correct answer is (A). Andrew's mother abruptly refused him to go possum hunting.

2. The correct answer is (A). As Mrs. Pearson was scolding Andrew not to go hunting, she mentioned she does not wish to see him go home with his arms shot off, head even.

3. The correct answer is (B). Mrs. Pearson was worried Andrew might get into an accident if he goes possum hunting with a gun.

4. The correct answer is (C). To make up your mind means to decide about something.

5. The correct answer is (D). Andrew already knew that his mother will not change her mind when she said no, but he tried boasting that he is not afraid of guns so that he can go hunting.

6. The correct answer is (D). To nip in the bud means to stop/halt something at an early stage, or thoroughly check something.

7. The correct answer is (C). To boast means to praise or express pride in one's own possessions, qualities, or accomplishments often to excess.

8. The correct answer is (B). The article is about the news on the recent discovery of twelve more of Jupiter's moons which took scientists about a year to confirm.

9. The correct answer is (A). The planet's moon count now stands at 92 which is the most in the solar system.

10. The correct answer is (C). Scott Sheppard, of the discovery team, said in the article that he thinks that more of them have yet to be found.

11. The correct answer is (D). According to the article, the new moons were spotted using telescopes and took scientists about a year to confirm.

12. The correct answer is (B). According to the article, the moons are small, no bigger than two miles across.

13. The correct answer is (A). To determine means to decide or to give an opinion about (something at issue or in dispute).

14. The correct answer is (A). An astronomer is a person who is skilled in astronomy or who makes observations of celestial phenomena. Astronomy is the study of objects and matter outside the Earth's atmosphere and of their physical and chemical properties.

15. The correct answer is (C). The article is about hole in Earth's ozone layer is on track to heal according to a new UN report.

16. The correct answer is (B). The gas in the ozone layer, ozone, shields the planet against harmful radiation from the sun which is linked to skin cancer and crop damage.

17. The correct answer is (D). A global agreement from 1987 led to a ban on chemicals in refrigerants and sprays that ate away the ozone layer.

18. The correct answer is (C). With current policies, ozone covering most of the planet could fully recover by 2040 and above Antarctica by 2066.

19. The correct answer is (B). To deplete means to lessen markedly in quantity, content, power, or value.

20. The correct answer is (C). With current policies on the deal of banning use of ozone-destroying chemicals, ozone covering most of the planet could fully recover by 2040 and above Antarctica by 2066.

21. The correct answer is (B). It will take until 2066 to fix the hole above Antarctica, the report says.

22. The correct answer is (A). The article was about the discovery of the world's oldest rune stone on January 17 in Norway with letters from an ancient Scandinavian language, which could have been carved 2,000 years ago.

23. The correct answer is (C). The stone was etched with letters from an ancient Scandinavian language, which could have been carved 2,000 years ago.

24. The correct answer is (D). According to the article, not all the marking on the stone make sense. Some of the letters spell Idiberug, which could be the name of a person or a family.

25. The correct answer is (A). The rune stone will be on show for a month at the Museum of Cultural History, Oslo.

26. The correct answer is (B). To etch means to cut (as letters or designs) on a hard surface. Synonyms are to engrave, inscribe, or carve.

27. The correct answer is (C). Kristel Zilmer is a professor at the University of Oslo, Norway, and was referred as she.

28. The correct answer is (D). Zilmer described the discovery as sensational, which meant that even was so remarkable that it causes great excitement and interest. Synonyms are amazing, thrilling, and revealing.

Section 4

Essay Writing

One sunny morning, Coco went out to the park to play. It was the first day of summer. He had been staying at home, so he was excited to finally come out and play.

The park is huge with many trees and flowers. All of the neighbors love to play at the park in summer. Coco met a lot his friends with their owners. It was a happy morning for everyone.

As he walked through the trees, something colorful caught his eyes. It had wings that resembled the colors of the flowers. Coco followed the flying object, but he could not reach it. Finally, the object stopped flying away as they reached the flowers at full bloom. The object flew on to Coco's nose as its wings reflected the light of the sun. It was a beautiful scene to look at.

He wondered what this object could be. Then, his owner came running to him as he exclaimed, "What a beautiful butterfly you got there, Coco!" "So, you're a butterfly," Coco said to himself as his eyes glistened at the butterfly on his nose. From that day forward, he decided that a butterfly is his most favorite thing at the park.

SSAT Elementary Level Exam 2

The
SSAT
+ Elementary

SECTION 1

QUANTITATIVE MATH

Time—30 minutes
30 Questions

Following each problem in this section, there are five suggested answers. Select the best answer from the five choices.

Example

5,413 – 4,827 =

(A) 586
(B) 596
(C) 696
(D) 1,586
(E) 1,686

Answer

● (B) (C) (D) (E)

The correct answer to this question is lettered A, so space A is marked.

1. Evaluate: $7 - 2\frac{3}{8}$

(A) $4\frac{3}{8}$ (B) $4\frac{5}{8}$ (C) $3\frac{5}{8}$ (D) $6\frac{7}{8}$ (E) $5\frac{1}{8}$

2. Which of the following statements is true?

(A) $(3 \times 1 + 7) \times 4 = 96$ (B) $(5 + 9 - 2) \div 3 = 3$ (C) $2(7 \div 1) \times 3 + 5 = 42$

(D) $3(2 - 6) + 11 - 4 = -4$ (E) $2(2 \div 1) \times 0 \times 4 = 0$

3. A square has an area of 144 cm^2. What is the perimeter of the square?

(A) 1 (B) 0.57 (C) 51 cm (D) 48 cm (E) 42 cm

4. Which of the following is closest to 9.456?

(A) 9.400 (B) 9.546 (C) 9.460 (D) 9.500 (E) 9.445

5. Three people can paint 5 houses in 14 days. How many people are needed to paint 10 houses in 28 days?

(A) 6 people (B) 4 people (C) 5 people (D) 7 people (E) cannot be determined

6. Darius has pet dogs and cats. The ratio of his dogs to cats is 1 to 2. Which of the following could NOT be the total number of dogs and cats?

(A) 30 (B) 18 (C) 14 (D) 24 (E) 33

7. Which of the following has the greatest value?

(A) 7654 (B) 4756 (C) 7465 (D) 6574 (E) 7564

8. When 91 is divided by 3, the remainder is the same as when 17 is divided by what number?

(A) 3 (B) 1 (C) 5 (D) 4 (E) 0

For questions 9 and 10, please refer to the data given below:

Antique Jewelry Collection (Each Δ represents 23 pieces)	
Rings	Δ Δ Δ Δ Δ Δ Δ
Bracelets	Δ Δ Δ Δ Δ
Necklaces	Δ Δ Δ Δ Δ Δ
Pair of Earrings	Δ Δ Δ Δ Δ Δ Δ Δ Δ Δ Δ

9. How many more rings are there than bracelets?

(A) 40 (B) 46 (C) 23 (D) 32 (E) 39

10. How many necklaces are there?

(A) 115 (B) 138 (C) 161 (D) 183 (E) 151

11. What is the area of the rectangle given below if $x = 2$?

$4x + 4$

$x - 1$

(A) 12 u^2 (B) 10 u^2 (C) 15 u^2 (D) 8 u^2 (E) 6 u^2

12. What is 59% of 1200?

(A) 717 (B) 720 (C) 704 (D) 708 (E) 710

13. The find value of x. $5463 - 4081 = x$

(A) 1823 (B) 1328 (C) 1382 (D) 1832 (E) 1238

14. A triangle has a base of 10 centimeters and a height of 12 centimeters. What is the area of the triangle?

(A) 45 cm^2 (B) 120 cm^2 (C) 60 cm^2 (D) 30 cm^2 (E) 90 cm^2

15. Which statement is true regarding line segments?

(A) a line segment is a "piece" of a line and has two endpoints

(B) a line segment has three endpoints

(C) a line segment is curved

(D) a line segment extends in both directions without endpoints

(E) a line segment has one endpoint but continues indefinitely in one direction

16. Mara has 7 marbles. There are 2 red, 3 blue, and 2 yellow. What is the probability that Maja will choose a red marble?

(A) $\frac{4}{7}$ (B) $\frac{3}{7}$ (C) $\frac{6}{7}$ (D) $\frac{2}{7}$ (E) $\frac{5}{7}$

17. Fill in the missing number in the pattern: 15, 21, 27, 33, ________, 45, 51

(A) 37 (B) 38 (C) 40 (D) 42 (E) 39

18. If there are 99 girls and 117 boys in a same grade level, what is the ratio of girls to boys in that grade level, in simplest form?

(A) 12:14 (B) 13:11 (C) 11:13 (D) 10:12 (E) 12:10

19. Solve for the variable $\frac{7}{12} = \frac{x}{24}$

(A) 28 (B) 14 (C) 7 (D) 16 (E) −24

20. Carla bought 5 snacks from the vending machine. If each snack costs \$3.52, how much money did Carla spent?

(A) \$17.00 (B) \$16.60 (C) \$16.70 (D) \$17.60 (E) \$17.50

21. In 5 years, Micha will be 14 years old. Her mother celebrated her birthday yesterday is now 4 times older than her current age. How old is her mother now?

(A) 36 years old (B) 30 years old (C) 32 years old (D) 38 years old (E) 33 years old

22. Lawrence just received a 13% increase in his weekly salary. If he now earns \$187.58 each week, what was his weekly salary before the pay raise?

(A) \$152 (B) \$145 (C) \$160 (D) \$156 (E) \$166

23. Mark has 10 shirts on his bed. 4 shirts are blue, 3 shirts are purple, 2 shirts are green, and 1 shirt is white. What is the chance that Mark randomly picks a purple shirt from the shirts on his bed?

(A) $\frac{4}{10}$ (B) $\frac{2}{10}$ (C) $\frac{3}{10}$ (D) $\frac{7}{10}$ (E) $\frac{1}{10}$

24. What is the area of the triangle?

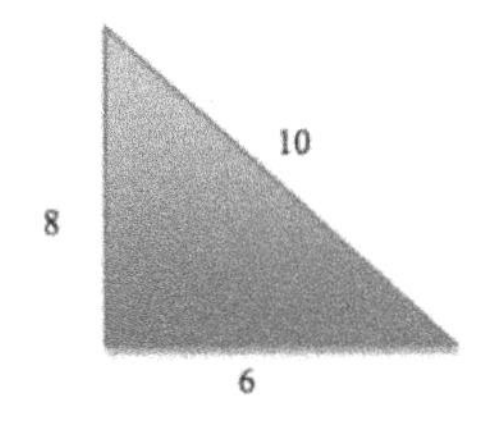

(A) 16 u^2 (B) 24 u^2 (C) 12 u^2 (D) 20 u^2 (E) 18 u^2

25. Line AC is 24 in long. If Point B is the midpoint of Line AC, how many inches long is Line BC?

(A) 12 in (B) 9 in (C) 15 in (D) 7 in (E) 10 in

26. Place the following numbers in ascending order: 24, 9, 58

(A) 58, 24, 9 (B) 24, 9, 58 (C) 9, 24, 58 (D) 24, 58, 9 (E) 9, 58, 24

27. Convert the fraction to a decimal, and round it off to the nearest hundredths place: $\frac{8}{15}$

(A) 0.62 (B) 0.51 (C) 0.35 (D) 0.53 (E) 0.56

28. Solve for the variable a: $\frac{5}{9} = \frac{a}{27}$

(A) 17 (B) 10 (C) 15 (D) 12 (E) 14

For questions 29 and 30, please refer to the problem given below:

Prince bought a balloon (that is a perfect sphere) with a radius of 2 cm. He wanted his balloon to be bigger, so he blew 2 big breaths of air into the balloon. Each big breath increased the balloon's radius by 1 cm.

29. What is the surface area of the balloon after Prince blew 2 big breaths of air?

(A) 72π cm^2 (B) 64π cm^2 (C) 50π cm^2 (D) 48π cm^2 (E) 44π cm^2

30. What is the ratio of the current volume of the balloon to the original volume of the balloon?

(A) 8 (B) 1 (C) 6 (D) 16 (E) 4

SECTION 2

VERBAL REASONING

Time—20 minutes
30 Questions

This section consists of two different types of questions. There are directions for each type.
Each of the following questions consists of one word followed by four words or phrases. You have to select a word or phrase whose meaning is closest to the word in capital letters.

Example

SWIFT: (A) clean (B) fancy (C) fast (D) quiet

Answer
Ⓐ Ⓑ ● Ⓓ

1. CONVENTIONAL

(A) extraordinary (B) unusual (C) exceptional (D) usual

2. INQUIRY

(A) answer (B) response (C) question (D) reply

3. SUSTAIN

(A) abandon (B) nurture (C) decline (D) reject

4. ROBUST

(A) healthy (B) weak (C) feeble (D) ill

5. IMPLY

(A) indicate (B) proclaim (C) declare (D) explain

6. DORMANT

(A) awake (B) resting (C) sleepless (D) conscious

7. ERADICATE

(A) protect (B) conserve (C) destroy (D) preserve

8. PROCURE

(A) lose (B) pay (C) grant (D) obtain

9. VEND

(A) sell (B) buy (C) purchase (D) procure

10. SOMBER

(A) dark (B) light (C) bright (D) luminous

11. REFRAIN

(A) restrain (B) concede (C) surrender (D) succumb

12. EXILE

(A) receive (B) repatriate (C) banish (D) shelter

13. FATHOM

(A) doubt (B) ignore (C) comprehend (D) forget

14. FLATTER

(A) disparage (B) praise (C) belittle (D) depreciate

15. FRAGILE

(A) delicate (B) strong (C) sturdy (D) tough

The following questions ask you to find the relationships between words. For each question, select the choice that best completes the meaning of the sentence.

Example

Ann carried the box carefully so that she would not _____ the pretty glasses.

(A) break (B) fix (C) open (D) stop

Answer

● (B) (C) (D)

16. Present is to past as now is to

(A) today (B) present (C) showing (D) later

17. Bottle is to glass as table is to

(A) chair (B) dining (C) kitchen (D) wood

18. Salt is to pepper as catsup is to

(A) bottle (B) tomato (C) mustard (D) red

19. Police is to criminal as driver is to

(A) male (B) taxi (C) passenger (D) cab

20. Banana is to yellow as apple is to

(A) fruit (B) red (C) crunchy (D) tree

21. Clock is to time as a ruler is to

(A) wood (B) length (C) plastic (D) kilograms

22. Generosity is to greed as kindness is to

(A) cruelty (B) benevolence (C) character (D) adjective

23. Water is to liquid as book is to

(A) solid (B) read (C) history (D) pages

24. Frog is to amphibian as tiger is to

(A) egg (B) mammal (C) stripe (D) jungle

25. Remote is to isolated as distinguished is to

(A) unknown (B) obscure (C) famous (D) anonymous

26. Seldom is to rarely as often is to

(A) frequently (B) never (C) sometimes (D) occasionally

27. Beautiful is to adjective as sometimes is to

(A) rarely (B) always (C) adverb (D) verb

28. Ring is to gold as coin is to

(A) change (B) currency (C) round (D) copper

29. Pentagon is to five as triangle is to

(A) three (B) shape (C) pyramid (D) right

30. Ship is to sea as airplane is to

(A) wings (B) sky (C) pilot (D) flight

SECTION 3

READING COMPREHENSION

Time—30 minutes
28 Questions

Read each passage carefully and answer the questions about it. For each question, decide on the basis of the passage which one of the choices best answers the questions.

When Dorothy stood in the doorway and looked around, she could see nothing but the great gray prairie on every side. Not a tree nor a house broke the broad sweep of flat country that reached the edge of the sky in all directions. The sun had baked the plowed land into a gray mass, with little cracks running through it. Even the grass was not green, for the sun had burned the tops of the long blades until they were the same gray color to be seen everywhere. Once the house had been painted , but the sun blistered the paint and the rains washed it away, and now the house was as dull and gray as everything else.

When Aunt Em came there to live, she was a young, pretty wife. The sun and wind had changed her, too. They had taken the sparkle from her eyes and left them a sober gray; they had taken away the red from her cheeks and lips, and they were gray also. She was thin and gaunt, and never smiled, now.

From The Wonderful Wizard of Oz *by L. Frank Baum*

1. How was the weather condition of where Dorothy lived described in the passage?

(A) suitable for farming with abundant source of water for crops (B) dry and hot

(C) cold wintery (D) tropical and breezy

2. What does the underlined word "prairie" mean?

(A) skyline (B) city (C) grassland (D) highway

3. After reading the passage, we may assume that Dorothy is

(A) vacationing in the countryside (B) a student from the countryside

(C) a farm girl (D) living with her Aunt Em

4. What does the underlined word "blistered" mean?

(A) cause an enclosed raised spot on the paint (B) to push upward

(C) repair the surface (D) investigate thoroughly

5. What part of speech is the underlined word "gaunt"?

(A) noun (B) verb (C) adjective (D) adverb

6. What does "had taken the sparkle in her eyes" mean in the passage mean?

(A) has blinded her eyes (B) has taken the enthusiasm in her eyes

(C) has caused blurry vision (D) developed a cataract

7. After reading the passage, we may assume that Aunt Em is

(A) determined (B) unhappy (C) jubilant (D) blissful

One frightfully hot morning, when she was about nine years old, she awakened feeling very cross, and she became crosser still when she saw that the servant who stood by her bedside was not her Ayah.

"Why did you come?" she said to the strange woman. "I will not let you stay. Send my Ayah to me."

The woman looked frightened, but she only stammered that the Ayah could not come.

"Is it so very bad? Oh, is it?" Mary heard her say.

"Awfully," the young man answered in a trembling voice. "Awfully, Mrs. Lennox. You ought to have gone to the hills two weeks ago."

At that very moment such a loud sound of wailing broke out of from the servants' quarters that she clutched the young man's arm, and Mary stood shivering from head to foot. The wailing grew wilder and wilder.

"What is it? What is it?" Mrs. Lennox gasped.

"Someone has died," answered the boy officer. "You did not say it had broken out among your servants."

From The Secret Garden *by Frances Hodgson Burnett*

8. As implied by the passage, what is an Ayah?

(A) a native maid or nursemaid (B) a relative (C) a teacher (D) mother

9. After reading the passage, we may assume that the reason Mary's Ayah could not come to her in the morning was

(A) she fell ill with the disease that broke out among the servants

(B) she got promoted to a higher-ranking position

(C) she was reassigned to a new mistress

(D) she didn't want to work anymore

10. What were the young officer and Mrs. Lennox talking about?

(A) they were having an affair (B) Mrs. Lennox planned on escaping from her husband

(C) the severity of the outbreak of the disease (D) not implied in the article

11. What does the underlined word "stammered" mean?

(A) cut, knock, or bring down (B) speak spontaneously

(C) murmur indistinctly (D) utter with involuntary stops or repetitions

12. What part of speech is the underlined word "someone"?

(A) pronoun (B) conjunction (C) adjective (D) adverb

13. After reading the passage, we may assume that Mary was

(A) a bright child (B) sick of the disease that broke out among the servants

(C) close to her Ayahs (D) afraid of her Ayah

14. How does Mrs. Lennox feel about the wailing sound?

(A) romantic (B) cheerful (C) frightened (D) emotional

On March 4, United Nations (U.N.) member countries agreed on a new treaty. It will protect marine life in the high seas. These are ocean waters outside of all national boundaries. The treaty will protect 30% of the world's oceans. That's nearly half of the planet's surface. More money will go toward conservation of those areas.

The treaty is a "success for international marine protection," says Steffi Lemke, Germany's environmental minister.

For years, the high seas have suffered because of commercial fishing and mining. Chemicals and plastics pollute the water. All of these harm the animal species that migrate through the high seas. The treaty is meant to protect these animals. It also protects coastal biodiversity. Many economies depend on it.

Malin Pinsky is a biologist at Rutgers University. "The ocean is not a limitless resource," he says, "and it requires global cooperation to use the ocean sustainably."

From New Ocean Treaty *by Brian S. McGrath, Time for Kids*

15. What is the article about?

(A) about the dangers of commercial fishing and mining

(B) about the new treaty agreed by UN member countries to protect marine life in the high seas from commercial fishing, mining, and chemicals and plastics which pollute the water

(C) about the national boundaries

(D) about the success of commercial fishing and mining industries

16. What is the objective of the new treaty?

(A) protect marine life in high seas which is 30% of the world's oceans

(B) protect commercial fishing and mining industries from getting out of business

(C) promote commercial fishing and mining

(D) drive economy up by supporting commercial fishing

17. What brought about the need to agree on a new treaty?

(A) it was about time to revisit the treaty as it has an expiration date

(B) nearly half of the planet's surface has been used as a resource in fishing so they are promoting to fish on other marine sites

(C) for years, the high seas have suffered because of commercial fishing and mining and chemicals and plastics which harmed the animal species that migrate through the high seas

(D) they needed something to do

18. Which among the words below is a synonym of the underlined word "limitless"?

(A) infinite (B) limited (C) little (D) scarce

19. Who participated in the new treaty?

(A) commercial fishing parties (B) UN member countries

(C) fish canning companies (D) small group of fishermen

20. Which among the choices below is not one of the objectives of the new ocean treaty?

(A) protect marine life in the high seas

(B) protect the animal species that migrate through the high seas

(C) protect coastal biodiversity

(D) protect commercial fishing and promote use of dynamite in fishing

21. When was the treaty agreed on?

(A) sometime in March (B) March 30 (C) March 14 (D) March 4

Biologist Paula Costa is standing in a field of red dirt. It's in São Paulo State, in Brazil. The land was once part of a rainforest called the Mata Atlântica. Today, nearly all of the forest has been cleared. Much of it is used for monoculture farming. That's when fields are planted with just one type of crop at a time.

The soil is hard and dry. Yet a few green shoots have popped up. The rainforest is making a comeback. "These will be jack beans," Costa says. "These are radishes. They're going to bring the soil back to life."

This is not just a reforestation project. It's also a farm. Soon, these crops will be joined by coffee plants and banana trees. There will be native trees. Some of the plants will pull nutrients to the topsoil with their roots. Most will produce crops to sell. "Everything has its function," Costa says.

Her partner is Valter Ziantoni. They run a project called Pretaterra. It teaches agroforestry. This farming method copies natural ecosystems. By 2025, the couple plans to spread it over a large part of what used to be the Mata Atlântica.

Agroforestry is a lot like how Indigenous people managed the land in Brazil long ago. But in the 20th century, the government began telling people to clear the rainforest and plant single crops. Farmers could earn money faster that way.

But clearing trees has caused problems. Brazil's rainforests preserve the wet climate that makes things grow. Trees take water into their roots and release it when the air around them is hot. This cools the landscape. With fewer trees, Brazil has become hotter and drier.

That's not good for farmers. Some see agroforestry as the solution. Growing trees alongside crops is like putting in an air conditioner and sprinklers. Ziantoni is excited about the future. "We want our impact on the landscape to be as big as possible," he says.

From Good Growing *by Ciara Nugent for TIME, adapted by TFK editors*

22. What is the main article about?

(A) about agroforestry and how it will help restore the rainforest in Brazil

(B) about starting monoculture farming and its advantages

(C) about planting one crop in the entire land all year round to make more money

(D) about the species of trees in Brazil's rainforest

23. As defined in the passage, what is monoculture farming?

(A) planting multiple crops (B) planting similar family of crops at a time

(C) planting with just one type of crop at a time (D) planting alternating crops per season

24. What were the disadvantages of monoculture farming in Brazil?

(A) they only had to tend to one kind of crop

(B) they did not have to think of that crop to plant

(C) farmers earn money faster

(D) when the trees were cleared up, Brazil became hotter and drier

25. What is agroforestry?

(A) growing trees alongside crops

(B) growing banana trees while waiting for the season to plant crops

(C) clearing the forest of trees

(D) not stated in the article

26. How does agroforestry help?

(A) it will slow down growth of crops

(B) trees act as air conditioner and sprinklers which cools the landscape where crops are planted

(C) it will provide shade when harvesting crops

(D) it will promote diversity in crops therefore more options

27. Based on the pronoun used for Ziantoni, we can assume that her gender is

(A) a child (B) a female (C) a male (D) unknown

28. What does the underlined word "impact" mean?

(A) a combination of qualities, such as shape, color, or form, which pleases the aesthetic senses, especially the sight

(B) an impression given by someone or something, although this may be misleading

(C) no longer fresh and pleasant to eat; hard, musty, or dry

(D) influence on someone or something

SECTION 4

WRITING SAMPLE

Time—15 minutes

Directions:

Write an essay on the following prompt on the paper provided. Your essay should not exceed two pages and must be written in ink. Erasing is not allowed.

Look at the picture and write a story about what happened. Be sure your story includes a beginning, middle, and conclusion.

Answer Key

Section 1

1. B	6. C	11. A	16. D	21. A	26. C
2. E	7. A	12. D	17. E	22. E	27. D
3. D	8. D	13. C	18. C	23. C	28. C
4. C	9. B	14. C	19. B	24. B	29. B
5. A	10. B	15. A	20. D	25. A	30. A

1. Answer: **B**

   Let's make the expression into like terms. Convert the whole number into fractions. $\frac{7}{1} - \frac{19}{8}$. Find the LCM of the denominator, then subtract: $\frac{56}{8} - \frac{19}{8} = \frac{37}{8} = 4\frac{5}{8}$. The answer is B.

2. Answer: **E**

   Evaluate each option. Use the PEMDAS rule. For option A, $(3 \times 1 + 7) \times 4 = (3 + 7) \times 4 = 10 \times 4 = \underline{40}$.

   For option B, $(5 + 9 - 2) \div 3 = 12 \div 3 = \underline{4}$. For option C, $2(7 \div 1) \times 3 + 5 = 14 \times 3 + 5 = 42 + 3 = \underline{45}$. For option D, $3(2 - 6) + 11 - 4 = -12 + 7 = \underline{-5}$. For option E, $2(2 \div 1) \times 0 \times 4 = 0$. Among the choices, only option E was solved correctly, hence the answer is E.

3. Answer: **D**

   We need to get first the length of each side of the square. $A = s^2 \Rightarrow 144 = s^2 \Rightarrow s = 12$ cm. Now that we have the length of the side, we can solve for the perimeter. $P = 4s = 4(12) = 48$ cm. The perimeter is 48 cm, hence the answer is D.

4. Answer: **C**

   Round off the given number to the nearest tens and we'll get 9.460, hence the answer is C.

5. Answer: **A**

   If 3 people can paint 5 houses in 14 days, then it means that for painting 10 houses in 28 days we need 6 people. To paint 10 houses in 28 days, we need 6 people, hence the answer is A.

6. Answer: **C**

   If you add the ratio of dogs to cats, you will get 3. The total number of pets then should be divisible by 3. Among the choices, only option C is not divisible by 3, hence the answer is C

7. Answer: **A**

Among the choices, option A has the greatest value, hence the answer is A.

8. Answer: **D**

Let's get the value of the remainder first. When we divide 91 by 3, we will get 30 with remainder 1.

If we divide 17 with the choices given, then these will be the results: A. 5 remainder 2; B. 17 with no remainder; C. 3 remainder 2; D. 4 remainder 1; E. undefined. Among the choices, option C has the same remainder, hence the answer is D.

9. Answer: **B**

Each Δ represents 23 pieces. There are 7 Δ for the rings, and if we multiply it with 23, then there will 161 pieces total. There are 5 Δ for the bracelets, and if we multiply it with 23, there will be 115 pieces total. Subtract the total pieces of bracelets from the total pieces of rings: 161 – 115 = 46. There are 46 pieces more of rings than bracelets, hence the answer is B.

10. Answer: **B**

There are 6 Δ. Since each Δ represents 23 pieces, multiply it with the number of Δ given for the necklace: $6 \times 23 = 138$. There are 138 pieces of necklace, hence the answer is B.

11. Answer: **A**

Substitute the value of x to get the length and width: $4x + 4 = 4(2) + 4 = 8 + 4 = 12$; $x - 1 = 2 - 1 = 1$. We now have the length for 12 units and width for 1 unit. Find the area: $A = l \times w = 12 \times 1 = 12\ u^2$. The area is $12\ u^2$, hence the answer is A.

12. Answer: **D**

Multiply: $1200 \times \frac{59}{100} = 708$. The 59% of 1200 is 708, hence the answer is D.

13. Answer: **C**

Evaluate: $5463 - 4081 = 1382$. The value of x is 1382, hence the answer is C.

14. Answer: **C**

To get the area of a triangle, use the formula, $A = \frac{1}{2}bh$. Substitute with the values given for base and height: $A = \frac{1}{2}(10 \times 12) = 60$. The area of the triangle is 60 cm^2, hence the answer is C.

15. Answer: **A**

The definition of line segment is a piece of a line connected by two endpoints, hence the answer is A.

16. Answer: **D**

The total number of marbles is 7 and since there are 2 red marbles, the probability of getting a red marble is two out of seven or $\frac{2}{7}$, hence the answer is D.

17. Answer: **E**

The common difference of the sequence is 6, so add 6 to 33 to get the next number: $33 + 6 = 39$. The next number is 39, hence the answer is E.

18. Answer: **C**

The ratio of girls to boys is 99:117. Let's express the ratio to its simplest form. The LCM of 99 and 117 is 9. The simplest form of the ratio 99:117 is 11:13, hence the answer C.

19. Answer: **B**

Cross-multiply to get the value of x: $\frac{7}{12} = \frac{x}{24} \Rightarrow 12x = 168 \Rightarrow x = 14$. The value of x is 14, hence the answer is B.

20. Answer: **D**

Multiply the amount of each snack to the total number of snacks bought: $5 \times \$3.52 = \$17.60$. The total amount Carla spent is \$17.60, hence the answer is D.

21. Answer: **A**

Let x be the current age of Micha. Find the value of x: $x + 5 = 14 \Rightarrow x = 9$. Micha's current age is 9 years old. Her mother is 4 times older than her: $4 \times 9 = 36$. Her mother is 36 years old, hence the answer is A.

22. Answer: **E**

Let x be Lawrence's previous weekly salary. Since he has a 13% increase, he's now earning 113% of what he previously earned. Express this into an equation and solve for x. $113\%x = 187.58 \Rightarrow x = 166$. Lawrence was earning \$166.00 before the pay raise; hence the answer is E.

23. Answer: **C**

The total number of shirts is 10, and since there are 3 purple shirts, the probability of getting a purple shirt is three out of ten or $\frac{3}{10}$, hence the answer is C.

24. Answer: **B**

To get the area of the triangle, use the formula $A = \frac{1}{2}bh$. Substitute with the values given for base and height: $A = \frac{1}{2}(6 \times 8) = \frac{1}{2}(48) = 24$. The area of the triangle is 24 u^2, hence the answer is B.

25. Answer: **A**

The definition of midpoint of a line segment is the point on that line segment that divides the segment into two congruent segments. Point B divides Line AC into two equal parts, so we just need to divide the length of Line AC by two to get the length of Line BC: 24 ÷ 2 = 12. Line BC measures 12 in, hence the answer is A.

26. Answer: **C**

We need to rearrange the numbers from least to greatest order: 9, 24, 58, hence the answer is C.

27. Answer: **D**

To convert a fraction to its decimal, divide the numerator with the denominator. 8 ÷ 15 = 0.533333. Round it off to the nearest hundredths place, we will have 0.53, hence the answer is D.

28. Answer: **C**

Cross-multiply to get the value of a: $\frac{5}{9} = \frac{a}{27} \Rightarrow 9a = 135 \Rightarrow a = 15$. The value of a is 15, hence the answer is C.

29. Answer: **B**

The formula of the surface area of a sphere is $SA = 4\pi r^2$. After each big breath of air, the radius of the balloon increases by 1 cm, and since Prince blew 2 big breaths, there will be an increase of 2 cm. The new radius will be 4 cm. Substitute: $SA = 4\pi r^2 = 4\pi\,(4^2) = 64\pi$ cm^2. The surface area is 64π cm^2, hence the answer is B.

30. Answer: **A**

First, let's find the original volume of the balloon and the current volume. To get the volume of the balloon (which is a perfect sphere), use the formula $V = \frac{4}{3}\pi r^3$. Let's solve for the original volume (V_o). $V_o = \frac{4}{3}\pi r^3 = \frac{4}{3}\pi(2^3) = \frac{4}{3}\pi(8) = \frac{32}{3}\pi$. Now, let's solve for the current volume (V_c). $V_c = \frac{4}{3}\pi(4^3) = \frac{4}{3}\pi(64) = \frac{256}{3}\pi$. Let's divide the original volume from the current volume to find the ratio.

Volume ratio = $\frac{\textit{Current volume}}{\textit{Original volume}} = \frac{\frac{256\pi}{3}}{\frac{32\pi}{3}} = \frac{256\pi}{3} \times \frac{3}{32\pi} = \frac{256}{32} = 8$. The ratio of the current volume to the original volume of the balloon is 8, hence the answer is A.

Section 2

1. D	11. A	21. B
2. C	12. C	22. A
3. B	13. C	23. A
4. A	14. B	24. B
5. A	15. A	25. C
6. B	16. D	26. A
7. C	17. D	27. C
8. D	18. C	28. D
9. A	19. C	29. A
10. A	20. B	30. B

1. The correct answer is (D). Conventional means accepted, used, or practiced by most people. Synonyms are usual, customary, and standard.

2. The correct answer is (C). An inquiry is an act or instance of asking for information. Synonyms are request, question, and query.

3. The correct answer is (B). To sustain means to supply with nourishment. Synonyms are to nurture, satisfy, and nourish. It also means to experience, to endure, and to support.

4. The correct answer is (A). Robust means enjoying health and vigor. Synonyms are healthy, well, and strong.

5. The correct answer is (A). To imply means to convey an idea indirectly. Synonyms are to indicate, hint, and suggest.

6. The correct answer is (B). Dormant means being in a state of suspended consciousness. Synonyms are asleep, resting, and slumbering.

7. The correct answer is (C). To eradicate means to destroy all traces of. Synonyms are to erase, abolish, and destroy.

8. The correct answer is (D). To procure means to receive as return for effort. Synonyms are to earn, obtain, and garner.

9. The correct answer is (A). To vend means to offer for sale to the public. Synonyms are to sell, market, and retail.

10. The correct answer is (A). Somber means being without light or without much light. Synonyms are dark, murky, and gloomy. It also means solemn or causing or marked by an atmosphere lacking in cheer.

11. The correct answer is (A). To refrain means to keep oneself from doing, feeling, or indulging in something and especially from following a passing impulse.

12. The correct answer is (C). To exile means to force to leave a country. Synonyms are to banish, evict, and deport.

13. The correct answer is (C). To fathom means to penetrate and come to understand. Synonyms are to comprehend, understand, and grasp.

14. The correct answer is (B). To flatter means to praise too much. Synonyms are to adulate, praise, and commend.

15. The correct answer is (A). Fragile means easily broken. Synonyms are delicate, brittle, and frail.

16. The correct answer is (D). The first word pair is antonyms.

17. The correct answer is (D). The first word pair has an object–composition relationship. A bottle is made of glass while a table is made of wood.

18. The correct answer is (C). Salt and pepper are commonly paired condiments like catsup and mustard.

19. The correct answer is (C). The first word pair has profession–purpose relationship. The police catch the criminal as a driver drives for a passenger.

20. The correct answer is (B). The first word pair has an item–color relationship. A banana is yellow as an apple is red.

21. The correct answer is (B). The first word pair has an item–function relationship. A clock is used to tell time while a ruler is used to measure length.

22. The correct answer is (A). The first word pair is antonyms.

23. The correct answer is (A). The first word pair has a matter–property relationship. Water is liquid as a book is solid.

24. The correct answer is (B). The first word pair has an animal–classification relationship. A frog is an amphibian as a tiger is a mammal.

25. The correct answer is (C). The first word pair is synonyms.

26. The correct answer is (A). The first word pair is synonyms.

27. The correct answer is (C). The first word pair has a word–part of speech relationship.

28. The correct answer is (D). The first word pair has an object–composition relationship. A ring is made of gold while a coin is made of copper.

29. The correct answer is (A). A pentagon has five sides as a triangle has three.

30. The correct answer is (B). A ship sails in the sea as an airplane flies in the sky.

Section 3

1. B	11. D	21. D
2. C	12. A	22. A
3. D	13. C	23. C
4. A	14. C	24. D
5. D	15. B	25. A
6. C	16. A	26. B
7. B	17. C	27. C
8. A	18. A	28. D
9. A	19. B	
10. C	20. D	

1. The correct answer is (B). As described in the passage, everything turned gray due to heat of the sun. The land was cracked, and the grass was gray.

2. The correct answer is (C). A prairie is a grassland, or a broad area of level, or rolling treeless country.

3. The correct answer is (D). The passage described how Aunt Em was when she came to live there where Dorothy is, therefore, we can assume that she lives with Aunt Em.

4. The correct answer is (A). To blister means to cause an enclosed raised spot (as in paint or the surface of baked dough) resembling a blister.

5. The correct answer is (C). Gaunt is an adjective which means excessively thin and angular.

6. The correct answer is (B). A spark in someone's eyes is seen as a sign of one's vitality, enthusiasm, and determination. The passage also said that Aunt Em never smiled, now.

7. The correct answer is (B). The passage said that the sparkle in her eyes had been taken. It also said that Aunt Em never smiled, now.

8. The correct answer is (A). An Ayah is a native maid or nursemaid employed by Europeans in India.

9. The correct answer is (A). In the last few sentences of the passage, it was implied that the disease broke out among servants and the wailing signaled that someone died.

10. The correct answer is (C). It was implied in the passage that Mrs. Lennox was asking the young officer how bad it was until they heard the wailing from the servants' quarters, which meant that someone died possibly of the outbreak.

11. The correct answer is (D). To stammer means to make involuntary stops and repetitions in speaking. In this passage, the servant was frightened.

12. The correct answer is (A). Someone is a pronoun which means some person. In this passage, it meant some servant.

13. The correct answer is (C). It was said in the passage that Mary demanded for her Ayah when she saw that someone else was beside her.

14. The correct answer is (C). It was described that Mrs. Lennox clutched the young officer's arm while asking what the wailing was about.

15. The correct answer is (B). The article is about the new treaty agreed by UN member countries to protect marine life in the high seas. The high seas have suffered from commercial fishing, mining, and chemicals and plastics which pollute the water.

16. The correct answer is (A). The treaty will protect 30% of the world's oceans, which are ocean waters outside of all national boundaries.

17. The correct answer is (C). The treaty is meant to protect animals that migrate through the high seas which have been suffering because of commercial fishing and mining and pollution from plastics and chemicals.

18. The correct answer is (A). Limitless means without end, limit, or boundary.

19. The correct answer is (B). On March 4th, UN member countries agreed on a new treaty.

20. The correct answer is (D). A, B, and C are the goals of the new treaty.

21. The correct answer is (D). On March 4th, UN member countries agreed on a new treaty.

22. The correct answer is (A). The passage is about how they are restoring the barren rainforest caused by monoculture farming through agroforestry.

23. The correct answer is (C). The government told the people in Brazil to clear the rainforest and start monoculture farming, which means planting single crops.

24. The correct answer is (D). In monoculture farming, trees were cleared up to use the land for planting single crops. Trees take water into their roots and release it when the air around them is hot. With fewer trees, Brazil has become hotter and drier.

25. The correct answer is (A). Agroforestry is a lot like how Indigenous people managed the land in Brazil long ago, which is growing trees alongside crops. It is like putting in an air conditioner and sprinklers.

26. The correct answer is (B). Growing trees alongside crops is like putting in an air conditioner and sprinklers. The wet climate makes things grow. Trees take water into their roots and release it when the air around them is hot.

27. The correct answer is (C). The pronoun used for Ziantoni is "he."

28. The correct answer is (D). Impact means the effect or influence of one person, thing, or action on another. Synonyms are influence, impression, and footprint.

Section 4

Essay Writing

It was the first day of school. Michael was nervous because he didn't know anyone. His family had just moved over the summer break. His father got a job offer so they had to relocate.

Michael is an only child and has always had a hard time making friends. He is shy and always kept to himself. His only friend was his childhood best friend who lived next door. Now that they moved, Michael was anxious that he would not make any friends at his new school.

While waiting for the school bus, he saw two students waiting by the bus stop near his house. He wanted to greet them and introduce himself as a new student, but his mouth won't open. Sweat ran down his face as he grew more anxious looking at the bus getting nearer to the bus stop. He thought "If I can't say hello here, I might not be able to inside the bus with too many people around."

As he was about to open his mouth, he noticed the girl to his left was also nervously clenching her fist and sweating. He realized that he is not the only person who feels anxious when meeting new people or being in an unfamiliar environment. Then, he took the courage to say hi. He felt good and when he saw that the girl was no longer anxious, he felt even better. Michael said to himself, "Moving isn't bad at all."

SSAT Elementary Level Exam 3

The
SSAT
+ Elementary

SECTION 1

QUANTITATIVE MATH

Time—30 minutes
30 Questions

Following each problem in this section, there are five suggested answers. Select the best answer from the five choices.

Example:

$5,413 - 4,827 =$

(A) 586
(B) 596
(C) 696
(D) 1,586
(E) 1,686

Answer

● (B) (C) (D) (E)

The correct answer to this question is lettered A, so space A is marked.

1. If a is an odd number, which of the following will result to an even number?

(A) $12 + a$ (B) $(7 \times 0) + a$ (C) $(21 + a) - 2$ (D) $10 - (4 + a)$ (E) $8 + 2 + a$

2. Find the missing parts of the set: _____, _____, 99, 88, 77, 66

(A) 121, 110 (B) 222, 111 (C) 121, 101 (D) 100, 111 (E) 221, 110

3. Clara ordered a large pizza for their dinner tonight. It had 20 slices. If her mom ate 2 slices, her dad with 4 slices, her brother ate 3 slices, and her with 2 slices, how many slices are left?

(A) 10 (B) 8 (C) 5 (D) 9 (E) 12

4. Find the area of the rectangle.

(A) $12\ u^2$ (B) $14\ u^2$ (C) $22\ u^2$ (D) $20\ u^2$ (E) $24\ u^2$

5. What is 245% of 60?

(A) 145 (B) 147 (C) 150 (D) 152 (E) 155

6. Evaluate: 5674 – 1397 + 250

(A) 4257 (B) 4527 (C) 4275 (D) 4572 (E) 4725

7. A triangle has side of three different lengths. One of its sides is 15 in long. The second side is 11 in long. The third side is the average length of the other two sides. What is the perimeter of this triangle?

(A) 39 in (B) 30 in (C) 29 in (D) 40 in (E) 35 in

8. Lloyd's piggy bank contains an assortment of quarters, dimes, nickels, and pennies. Assuming that all coins are equally likely to be picked, what is the probability of drawing a nickel if there are 10 quarters, 13 dimes, 22 nickels, and 5 pennies?

(A) 40% (B) 20% (C) 44% (D) 10% (E) 26%

For questions 9 and 10, please refer to the table below:

Student Name	Math Test Score
Fiona	84
Lee	91
Arthur	82
Sandy	93
Michelle	90

9. What is the average math test score of the five students?

(A) 87 (B) 89 (C) 91 (D) 88 (E) 90

10. Who got the highest math test score?

(A) Lee (B) Arthur (C) Fiona (D) Michelle (E) Sandy

11. Bill ate two chocolate muffins each day from Monday to Friday. How many muffins did he eat in all?

(A) 2 muffins (B) 5 muffins (C) 8 muffins (D) 10 muffins (E) 12 muffins

12. Which sequence below follows the rule of adding 7?

(A) 15, 25, 35, 45 (B) 10, 17, 25, 34 (C) 12, 19, 26, 33 (D) 9, 16, 22, 27 (E) 4, 8, 12, 16

13. A $75 jacket is on sale for $45. What percentage of the original price has been discounted for the sale?

(A) 40% (B) 30% (C) 20% (D) 10% (E) 0%

14. Evaluate: $894 \div 50$

(A) 17.88 (B) 17.89 (C) 17.99 (D) 17.98 (E) 17.17

15. Find the perimeter of the figure below:

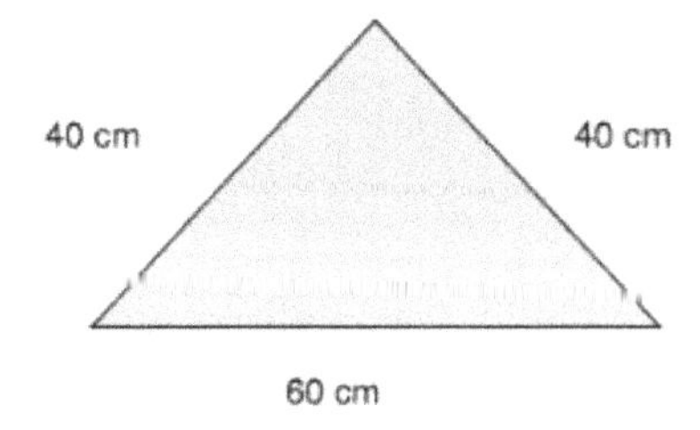

(A) 138 cm (B) 140 cm (C) 130 cm (D) 135 m (E) 145 cm

16. Patrick got a \$150 gift card from his parents to his favorite clothing store. He bought a shirt that costs \$38, a pair of pants that costs \$41, and a hat that costs \$16. How much does he have left?

(A) \$60 (B) \$55 (C) \$65 (D) \$58 (E) \$52

17. Which statement is true?

(A) $349 < 319$ (B) $339 = 329$ (C) $329 > 359$ (D) $345 = 345$ (E) $309 < 300$

18. In the first week of December, 53 pine trees were cut down in a tree lot to use as a Christmas tree. If the tree lot has 105 pine trees initially, how many trees were left?

(A) 48 (B) 49 (C) 50 (D) 51 (E) 52

19. What is the missing number in the sequence?

92, 82, 72, _____, 52, 42

(A) 42 (B) 62 (C) 32 (D) 102 (E) 72

20. Order the objects from longest to shortest. The snake stuffed toy is 20 in long, the cat stuffed toy is 12 in long, the dog stuffed toy is 16 in long, and the tiger stuffed toy is 10 in long.

(A) snake, dog, tiger, cat (B) snake, cat, tiger, dog

(C) snake, dog, cat, tiger (D) snake, tiger, cat, dog (E) snake, cat, dog, tiger

21. John has a standard deck of cards. What is the probability that he will randomly select a black card from the deck?

(A) 51% (B) 52.5% (C) 48% (D) 50% (E) 42.5%

22. A triangle has a base of 6 cm and a height of 8 cm. What is the area of the triangle?

(A) 21 cm^2 (B) 25 cm^2 (C) 22 cm^2 (D) 24 cm^2 (E) 20 cm^2

23. Convert the given fraction to decimal: $\frac{5}{8}$

(A) 0.635 (B) 0.625 (C) 0.652 (D) 0.562 (E) 0.526

24. Karen has ten homework to do each week. If she does two homework per day, how many days each week will she have no homework to do?

(A) 4 (B) 0 (C) 3 (D) 1 (E) 2

25. My math teacher brought 54 pieces of chocolates. There are 9 of us students in the class. If my teacher gives each student the same number of chocolates, how many did each of us receive?

(A) 0 (B) 3 (C) 6 (D) 9 (E) 12

26. Derrick saw 10 birds sitting on a tree branch. Four flew away. Then three more flew away. How many birds are on the tree branch now?

(A) 1 (B) 4 (C) 7 (D) 3 (E) all flew away

For questions 27–30, refer to table below.

Student Name	Math Test Score	English Test Score	Science Test Score
Paula	85	90	88
Kenneth	92	89	90
Claude	90	93	90
Lina	88	93	90
Zoe	87	89	88

27. Which student has the greatest sum of their three-test score?

(A) Paula (B) Zoe (C) Lina (D) Claude (E) Kenneth

28. What was Claude average test score?

(A) 91 (B) 90.5 (C) 92 (D) 89.5 (E) 90

29. Which test subject did Claude get the highest test score?

(A) science (B) math (C) English (D) science and math (E) all scores are equal

30. Which test subject did Kenneth get the highest score?

(A) science (B) English (C) math (D) science and English (E) all scores are equal

SECTION 2

VERBAL REASONING

Time—20 minutes
30 Questions

This section consists of two different types of questions. There are directions for each type.

Each of the following questions consists of one word followed by four words or phrases. You have to select a word or phrase whose meaning is closest to the word in capital letters.

Example

SWIFT: (A) clean (B) fancy (C) fast (D) quiet

Answer
Ⓐ Ⓑ ● Ⓓ

1. FURIOUS
   (A) quiet (B) calm (C) mad (D) relaxed

2. GRACEFUL
   (A) elegant (B) clumsy (C) gawky (D) awkward

3. HAZARD
   (A) danger (B) protection (C) ward (D) shield

4. MERGE
   (A) separate (B) divide (C) split (D) combine

5. NAG
   (A) delight (B) whine (C) rejoice (D) tolerate

6. OCCUPY
   (A) desert (B) inhabit (C) bore (D) weary

7. SEQUENCE
   (A) reason (B) disorder (C) order (D) factor

8. UPROOT

(A) instill (B) insert (C) install (D) pull

9. VIGOROUS

(A) energetic (B) feeble (C) sluggish (D) weak

10. COMICAL

(A) funny (B) serious (C) lame (D) solemn

11. ORCHARD

(A) garage (B) highway (C) sidewalk (D) farm

12. SALVAGE

(A) jeopardize (B) save (C) compromise (D) risk

13. VALIANT

(A) cowardly (B) brave (C) craven (D) timid

14. BARRIER

(A) portal (B) opening (C) obstacle (D) entrance

15. ZANY

(A) sensible (B) clever (C) wise (D) foolish

The following questions ask you to find the relationships between words. For each question, select the choice that best completes the meaning of the sentence.

Example

Ann carried the box carefully so that she would not _____ the pretty glasses.

(A) break (B) fix (C) open (D) stop

Answer

● Ⓑ Ⓒ Ⓓ

16. Mock is to real as copy is to

(A) reproduce (B) original (C) cheat (D) carbon

17. Math is to equations as Science is to

(A) book (B) subject (C) elements (D) doctor

18. Cat is to dog as moon is to

(A) sun (B) round (C) night (D) crater

19. Food scrap is to biodegradable as plastic bottle is to

(A) clear (B) trash (C) drink (D) non-biodegradable

20. Clever is to wise as silly is to

(A) smart (B) decision (C) face (D) foolish

21. Carla is to girl as Brandon is to

(A) boy (B) name (C) gender (D) kid

22. Ant is to drone as antelope is to

(A) mammal (B) horn (C) buck (D) fast

23. Chicken is to hen as hamster is to

(A) doe (B) sunflower seeds (C) mammal (D) marsupial

24. Sky is to blue as grass is to

(A) short (B) sharp (C) green (D) garden

25. Hut is to straw as building is to

(A) tall (B) concrete (C) big (D) city

26. Needle is to nest as to octagon is to

(A) merry (B) never (C) orange (D) palm

27. Jellyfish is to noun as banish is to

(A) accept (B) expel (C) adverb (D) verb

28. Writer is to book as journalist is to

(A) television (B) person (C) smart (D) news

29. Square is to four as circle is to

(A) three (B) 0 (C) two (D) shape

30. Mailman is to mail as paperboy is to

(A) newspaper (B) young (C) early (D) run

SECTION 3

READING COMPREHENSION

Time—30 minutes
28 Questions

Read each passage carefully and answer the questions about it. For each question, decide on the basis of the passage which one of the choices best answers the questions.

Some leaves of a tree had been found on the nursery floor, which certainly were not there when the children went to bed, and Mrs. Darling was puzzling over them when Wendy said with a tolerant smile:

"I do believe it is that Peter again!"

"Whatever do you mean, Wendy?"

"It is so naughty of him not to wipe," Wendy said, sighing. She was a tidy child.

She explained in quite a matter-of-fact way that she thought Peter sometimes came to the nursery in the night and sat on the foot of her bed and played on his pipes to her. Unfortunately, she never woke, so she didn't know how she knew, she just knew.

"What nonsense you talk, precious! No one can get into the house without knocking."

From Peter and Wendy *by J.M. Barrie*

1. Which word best describes how Mrs. Darling felt about what Wendy said?

(A) disbelief (B) amusement (C) worry (D) anger

2. What is a nursery as used in the story?

(A) a place or natural habitat that breeds or supports animals

(B) a room in a house for the special use of young children

(C) a place where young plants and trees are grown for sale or for planting elsewhere

(D) school

3. Based on the pronoun used for Peter, we can assume that he is a

(A) infant (B) girl (C) boy (D) grandfather

4. What does the underlined word "naughty" mean?

(A) obedient (B) energetic (C) careful (D) mischievous

5. Which word is a synonym of "tidy"?

(A) messy (B) unkempt (C) shabby (D) neat

6. What does "matter-of-fact way" mean in the passage?

(A) full of feelings

(B) with flowing the enthusiasm in her eyes

(C) being plain, straightforward, or unemotional

(D) developed a plausible story

7. True or false. Mrs. Darling believes that Peter exists.

(A) true (B) false (C) maybe (D) unknown

The world population reached 8 billion in November, according to the United Nations (U.N.). This milestone was not unexpected. And it shows some good news: People are living longer, thanks in part to better health-care. Still, population growth poses a danger in many parts of the world.

A fair amount of the growth has been in the world's poorer countries, especially in Africa. The trend will strain resources in these places. "The housing, roads, the hospitals, schools—everything is overstretched," says Gyang Dalyop, who works in urban planning in Nigeria.

Other places with rapid growth include India, Pakistan, and the Philippines. Growing populations will make life harder in these places when combined with climate change. Less water and decreased crop production will mean more hungry people.

Experts say the problem lies mainly with richer countries, like the United States and China. These countries consume the most energy and produce the most greenhouse-gas emissions. "Population is not the problem," says Charles Kenny of the Center for Global Development, in Washington, D.C. "The way we consume is the problem."

From Population Rise *by Brian S. McGrath, Time for Kids*

8. What is the article about?

(A) the danger population growth poses and why

(B) how different each nation's population growth is

(C) who is to be blamed for climate change

(D) call for everyone to stop reproducing

9. After reading the article, what is the bigger problem behind the increase in population?

(A) according to Charles Kenny of the Center for Global Development, the problem is the way we consume and not the population

(B) the trend will strain resources and will make life harder for poorer countries

(C) there will be more hungry people

(D) all the above

10. Where was the increase in population attributed to?

(A) better healthcare

(B) fountain of youth

(C) life-prolonging grain variety

(D) not implied in the article

11. Why does population growth pose a danger in many parts of the world?

(A) the trend will strain resources in these places

(B) the housing, roads, the hospitals, schools—everything is overstretched

(C) both A and B

(D) none of the above

12. What does the underlined word "milestone" mean?

(A) lowlight (B) highlight (C) insignificant event (D) theory

13. Which is a synonym of the word "overstretched"?

(A) just enough (B) beyond normal limits (C) abundant supply (D) unlimited

14. What is the root cause of climate change as discussed in the article?

(A) richer countries consume the most energy and produce the most greenhouse-gas emissions

(B) poorer countries produce the most waste

(C) more populated countries consume the most energy

(D) not discussed in the article

Scientists have found that floating solar panels could provide a huge amount of electricity if they were placed on lakes and other bodies of water around the world. Floating solar panels could also help save water and protect land.

Solar panels—also known as "photovoltaic" panels—are used to turn sunlight into electricity. Most solar panels are placed on land in large collections called solar farms. But recently people have begun to explore putting floating solar panels on water. Because these panels float, some people call them "floatovoltaics."

The researchers behind the new study looked at 114,555 reservoirs worldwide. They used computer programs to figure out how much electricity could be produced yearly by covering 30% of these reservoirs with floating solar panels.

The answer was surprisingly large—more than twice the amount of energy the United States generates in a year.* And 10 times as much energy as all the solar power currently being generated in the world. One of the authors of the paper described the results as "remarkable."

Floatovoltaics can also help save water by limiting evaporation from reservoirs. The scientists say that solar panels covering just 30% of the reservoirs' surfaces could save as much water as 300,000 people would use in a year. As areas around the world struggle with droughts, many places are eager to save water in any way they can.

Putting solar panels on water also means that there's no need to clear land for a solar farm. That's more and more important as countries work to fight climate change and protect natural spaces for wild animals.

From Floating Solar Panels—Making Energy, Saving Water *by NFK Editors, News for Kids.net*

15. What is the article about?

(A) about the latest trend on solar panels attached to house roofs and how efficient they are

(B) about the inefficiency of solar panels to generate electricity compared to fuel-powered engines

(C) about the recent trend on floating solar panels and how more advantageous they are compared to ones on ground

(D) about how it's easier to generate electricity through animal fossils

16. How different are the floating solar panels from the ones on the ground?

(A) Not much. They are the same solar panels which are already waterproof but are placed on bodies of water instead of installed on the ground.

(B) they are specifically created to be submerged underwater

(C) they run underwater like a submarine and move to various parts of the ocean

(D) not specified in the article

17. What are the advantages of floating solar panels?

(A) helps save water by limiting evaporation

(B) helps save land since there's no need to clear land for a solar farm

(C) generates more electricity since there are more bodies of water in the world compared to land

(D) all the above

18. Which among the words below is a synonym of the underlined word "remarkable"?

(A) standard (B) impressive (C) subtle (D) scarce

19. What is the meaning of the underlined word "drought"?

(A) the opulence of prerevolutionary monarchs

(B) a period of abundance in harvest

(C) a period of dryness especially when prolonged

(D) spring and harvest time

20. After reading the article, will you say that floating solar panel is better?

(A) yes, because solar panels help save water by limiting evaporation and save land since there's no need to clear land for a solar farm. In addition, it generates more energy

(B) no, because there is no significant difference in the energy floating panels generate compared to the ground ones

(C) maybe, but I will need evidence

(D) I can't say

21. True or false. More electricity is generated by the floating solar panels compared to the ones on ground.

(A) false (B) true (C) maybe (D) I guess

Nobody likes to lose money. But if you happen to drop some cash by accident, Tokyo, Japan may be one of the best places to do it. Tokyo police report that last year, people turned in a record-breaking amount of lost money—roughly $29.6 million in cash.

In Japan, people are expected to turn in any lost money that they find. It's actually a law. But the country also has a reward system for people who turn in money they find.

If someone claims money that has been turned in, the finder can get a reward worth up to 20% of the money. And, after three months, if no one has claimed the money, the finder gets to keep it all.

But even so, the amount of money turned in in Tokyo last year set a record. The total was 3.99 billion Japanese yen, or about $29.6 million. That's about $1.1 million more than the previous record, which was set in 2019. On average, people in Tokyo found and turned in about $81,000 every day last year.

Tokyo is the capital of Japan. It's home to nearly 14 million people, and it's a hugely busy place. So, it's no wonder that lots of things get lost there.

So why was last year a record for cash? The Tokyo police don't think it was because people were more careless. They think it's because the coronavirus pandemic is ending. As Japan got the virus under better control, the country changed its rules to allow more visitors. Many more people began going out and doing more things.

From Tokyo: A Good Place to Lose Things *by NFK Editors, News for Kids.net*

22. What is the article about?

(A) about the increase in last year's amount of lost money reported in Tokyo, Japan and how people are expected to turn in these lost money

(B) about how unlucky you will be if you lose your money especially in Tokyo, Japan

(C) about tips on how to avoid losing money when travelling to Tokyo, Japan

(D) about how dangerous it is to travel to Tokyo, Japan because of pickpockets

23. As discussed in the article, why was last year's Tokyo police report of lost money record-breaking?

(A) they couldn't keep track of it anymore

(B) it summed up to roughly $29.6 million in cash, about $1.1 million more than the previous record in 2019

(C) it was three times more daily

(D) the conversion rate is higher than last year

24. Why are people in Tokyo expected to return lost items?

(A) it is in their law (B) there is a reward system (C) both A and B (D) none of the above

25. What happens if someone from Tokyo turns in any lost money?

(A) they get a reward

(B) the finder could get up to 20% of the money

(C) after three months, the finder will keep all the money if no one has claimed it

(D) all of the above

26. To which does the increase in loss of money attributed to?

(A) coronavirus pandemic was ending, and they got the virus under better control

(B) they allowed more visitors and changed its rules

(C) more people are going out and doing things

(D) all the above

27. True or false. The finder will keep the money if nobody claims it after three weeks.

(A) true (B) yes (C) false (D) unknown

28. What does the underlined word "record-breaking" mean?

(A) commonly seen (B) beyond any previous record

(C) within the expected outcome (D) no significance

SECTION 4

WRITING SAMPLE

Time—15 minutes

Directions:

Write an essay on the following prompt on the paper provided. Your essay should not exceed two pages and must be written in ink. Erasing is not allowed.

Look at the picture and write a story about what happened. Be sure your story includes a beginning, middle, and conclusion.

Answer Key

Section 1

1. C	6. B	11. D	16. B	21. A	26. D
2. A	7. A	12. C	17. D	22. D	27. D
3. D	8. C	13. A	18. E	23. B	28. A
4. E	9. E	14. A	19. B	24. E	29. C
5. B	10. E	15. B	20. C	25. C	30. C

1. Answer: **C**

   Let's substitute *a* with number 3. Option A: 12 + 3 = 15; Option B: (7 × 0) + 3 = 0 + 3 = 3; Option C: (21 + 3) – 2 = 24 – 2 = 22; Option D: 10 – (4 + 3) = 10 – 7 = 3; Option E: 8 + 2 + 3 = 13. Among the choices, only Option C resulted in an even number, hence the answer is C.

2. Answer: **A**

   Notice that the set is counting down/backward. If you look at how the numbers are related, you will notice that these numbers decrease by 11 or has multiples of 11. To solve, you can add 11 to the first known number (99) and then 11 to that number to find the first number in the sequence. You will then have a complete sequence of 121, 110, 99, 88, 77, 66, hence the answer is A.

3. Answer: **D**

   Let's add all the slices that were eaten by Clara's family and then subtract the result from the initial total slices to get the leftover slices: 2 + 4 + 3 + 2 = 11. 20 – 11 = 9. The total slices left were 9, hence the answer is D.

4. Answer: **E**

   To get the area of rectangle, use the formula $A = l \times w$. $A = 12 \times 2 = 24$. The area is 24 u^2, hence the answer is E.

5. Answer: **B**

   Multiply: $\frac{245}{100} \times 60 = 147$. That is, 245% of 60 is 147, hence the answer is B.

6. Answer: **B**

   Simplify the given equation from left to right: 5674 – 1397 + 250 = 4527. The answer is B.

7. Answer: **A**

To get the perimeter of the triangle, use the formula $P = s + s + s$. The lengths of the two sides are already given: 15 in and 11 in, we just need to find the length of the third side. It was given that the third side is the average length of the other two, so $\frac{15+11}{2} = \frac{26}{2} = 13$ in. Now that we got the length of the third side, solve for the perimeter. $P = 15 + 11 + 13 = 39$ in. The perimeter of the triangle is 39 in, hence the answer is A

8. Answer: **C**

Let's first get the total number of coins in the piggy bank. There are 10 quarters, 13 dimes, 22 nickels, and 5 pennies: $10 + 13 + 22 + 5 = 50$. There are 50 coins. To get the probability of randomly getting a nickel, divide the number of nickels by the total number of coins: $\frac{22}{50} = 0.44$ or 44%, hence the answer is C.

9. Answer: **E**

To get the average test score, add all the test scores and then divide it with total number of those scores given: $\frac{84+91+82+93+90}{5} = \frac{440}{5} = 88$. The average score is 88, hence the answer is E.

10. Answer: **E**

The highest score is 93, which is Sandy's score, hence the answer is E.

11. Answer: **D**

There are five days from Monday to Friday. Since he eats two muffins each day, multiply two with the total days from Monday to Friday: $2 \times 5 = 10$. He ate 10 muffins in total, hence the answer is D.

12. Answer: **C**

Choose the option that has a difference of 7 from the next number. Among the choices, only option C follows this rule, hence the answer is C.

13. Answer: **A**

Set up a proportion of the new price to the old price to see how they relate. $\frac{\$45}{\$75} = \frac{3}{5}$ of the original price. Subtract $\frac{3}{5}$ from 1 to find the amount that was discounted. $1 - \frac{3}{5} = \frac{2}{5} = 0.40$ or 40%. The percentage of the original price that has been discounted for the sale is 40%, hence the answer is A.

14. Answer: **A**

Divide: $894 \div 50 = 17.88$. The answer is A.

15. Answer: **B**

To get the perimeter of the triangle, use the formula $P = s + s + s = 40 + 40 + 60 = 140$. The perimeter is 140 cm, hence the answer is B.

16. Answer: **B**

Let's first get Patrick's total spendings and then subtract it from the total amount of the gift card. 150 – (38 + 41 + 16) = 150 – 95 = 55. Patrick still has $55 left, hence the answer is B.

17. Answer: **D**

Among the choices, only option D is correct, hence the answer is D.

18. Answer: **E**

Subtract the pine trees that were cut down from the total trees in the tree lot to get the number of pine trees left, 105 – 53 = 52. There are 52 pine trees left, hence the answer is E.

19. Answer: **B**

The sequence has a difference of 10. Subtract 10 from 72 to get the next number. 72 – 10 = 62. The missing number is 62, hence the answer is B.

20. Answer: **C**

When ordering from longest to shortest, compare the given lengths. The highest number will always be the longest. In this case, the number 20 is higher than 12, so the snake stuffed toy is longer than the cat stuffed toy. 16 is higher than 12, so the dog stuffed toy is longer that the cat stuffed toy. 10 is the lowest number, so the tiger stuffed is the shortest. The order is snake, dog, cat, tiger, hence the answer is C.

21. Answer: **D**

A standard deck of cards has 52 cards, 26 of which are black and 26 of which are red. To get the probability of getting one black card is 26 out 52: $\frac{black\,cards}{total\,cards} = \frac{26}{52} = \frac{1}{2}$ or 50%. The probability of getting a black card is 50%, hence the answer is D.

22. Answer: **D**

To get the area of a triangle, use the formula $A = \frac{1}{2}(b \times h) = \frac{1}{2}(6 \times 8) = \frac{1}{2}(48) = 24\text{ cm}^2$. The area of the triangle is 24 cm^2, hence the answer is D.

23. Answer: **B**

To convert a fraction to its decimal form, divide the numerator by the denominator: 5 ÷ 8 = 0.625. The decimal form of $\frac{5}{8}$ is 0.625, hence the answer is B.

24. Answer: **E**

Let's first divide the 10 homework by 2, since she will do two homework per day. 10 ÷ 2 = 5. Karen will have 5 days to do her homework. Since there are 7 days in a week, subtract the number of homework days from the number of days in a week: 7 – 5 = 2. She will have 2 non-homework days, hence the answer is E.

25. Answer: **C**

Divide the total number of chocolates by the total number of students: 54 ÷ 9 = 6. Each student will receive 6 chocolates, hence the answer is C.

26. Answer: **D**

Subtract; start from 10 birds. Four flew away: 10 – 4 = 6. Then another three flew away: 6 – 3 = 3. There are 3 birds remaining on the tree branch, hence the answer is D.

27. Answer: **D**

Add the test scores of each student. Paula: 85 + 90 + 88 = 263; Kenneth: 92 + 89 + 90 = 271; Claude: 90 + 93 + 90 = 273; Lina: 88 + 93 + 90 = 271; Zoe: 87 + 89 + 88 = 264. Claude has the highest test score with 272 total score, hence the answer is D.

28. Answer: **A**

To get the average score, add all Claude's scores, then divide it by the total number of test subjects. $\frac{90+93+90}{3}=\frac{273}{3}=91$. Claude's average test score is 91, hence the answer is A.

29. Answer: **C**

The highest score Claude got is 93, which is the English test, hence the answer is C.

30. Answer: **C**

The highest score Kenneth got is 92, which is the math test, hence the answer is C.

Section 2

1. C	11. D	21. A
2. A	12. B	22. C
3. A	13. B	23. A
4. D	14. C	24. C
5. B	15. D	25. B
6. B	16. B	26. C
7. C	17. C	27. D
8. D	18. A	28. D
9. A	19. D	29. B
10. A	20. D	30. A

1. The correct answer is (C). Furious means exhibiting or goaded by anger. Synonyms are mad, frantic, and fierce.

2. The correct answer is (A). Graceful means displaying grace in form or action : pleasing or attractive in line, proportion, or movement. Synonyms are agile, elegant, and majestic.

3. The correct answer is (A). Hazard means something that may cause injury or harm. Synonyms are danger, threat, and risk.

4. The correct answer is (D). To merge means to turn into a single mass or entity that is the same throughout. Synonyms are to combine, mix, and blend.

5. The correct answer is (B). To nag means to express dissatisfaction, pain, or resentment usually tiresomely. Synonyms are to complain and whine.

6. The correct answer is (B). To occupy means to take up (a place or extent in space). It also means to hold the attention of. Synonyms are to inhabit, engage, and distract.

7. The correct answer is (C). A sequence is a series of things linked together. It also means the way objects in space or events in time are arranged or follow one another. Synonyms are chain, string, and order.

8. The correct answer is (D). To uproot means to draw out by force or with effort. Synonyms are to pull, pry, and yank.

9. The correct answer is (A). Vigorous means having active strength of body or mind. Synonyms are energetic, robust, and dynamic.

10. The correct answer is (A). Comical means causing or intended to cause laughter. Synonyms are humorous, comedic, and funny.

11. The correct answer is (D). An orchard is a place where people grow fruit trees. Synonyms are garden, farm, and vineyard.

12. The correct answer is (B). To salvage means to remove (something) from a place of danger or harm. Synonyms are to rescue, recover, and save.

13. The correct answer is (B). Valiant means feeling or displaying no fear by temperament. Synonyms are brave, gallant, and courageous.

14. The correct answer is (C). A barrier is a physical object that blocks the way. Synonyms are wall, fence, barricade, and obstacle.

15. The correct answer is (D). Zany means showing or marked by a lack of good sense or judgment. Synonyms are silly, absurd, and foolish.

16. The correct answer is (B). The first word pair is an antonym. The opposite of a copy is the original.

17. The correct answer is (C). The first word pair has general category–specific relationship. Elements are studied in science as well as equations in math.

18. The correct answer is (A). The first word pair are common opposites. The moon is seen at night while the sun is seen during the day. Cats and dogs are seen to be natural enemies.

19. The correct answer is (D). The first word pair has item–category relationship. Plastic bottles are non-biodegradable wastes.

20. The correct answer is (D). The first word pair is a synonym.

21. The correct answer is (A). The first word pair has a name–gender relationship. Brandon is generally a boy's name.

22. The correct answer is (C). The first word pair has an animal–male name relationship. The male antelope is called a buck while a male ant is called a drone.

23. The correct answer is (A). The first word pair has an animal–female name relationship. The female hamster is called a doe while a female chicken is called a hen.

24. The correct answer is (C). The first word pair has an object–color relationship.

25. The correct answer is (B). The first word pair has object–material relationship. A hut is made of straw while a building is made of concrete.

26. The correct answer is (C). The first word pair has the same beginning letter.

27. The correct answer is (D). The first word pair has word–part of speech relationship.

28. The correct answer is (D). The first word pair has profession–product relationship. A writer authors a book while a journalist delivers the news.

29. The correct answer is (B). The first word pair has shape–sides relationship. A square has four sides while a circle has none.

30. The correct answer is (A). The first word pair has job–product relationship. A mailman delivers the mail while a paperboy delivers the newspaper.

Section 3

1. A	11. C	21. B
2. B	12. B	22. A
3. C	13. B	23. B
4. D	14. A	24. C
5. D	15. C	25. D
6. C	16. A	26. D
7. B	17. D	27. C
8. A	18. B	28. B
9. D	19. C	
10. A	20. A	

1. The correct answer is (A). In the last sentence, Mrs. Darling said in response to Wendy's story about Peter going through the window, "What nonsense you talk, precious! No one can get into the house without knocking."

2. The correct answer is (B). In the story, the nursery referred to is a room in a house for the special use of young children. This is where Wendy sleeps in her bed.

3. The correct answer is (C). The pronoun used to refer to Peter is "him."

4. The correct answer is (D). Naughty means engaging in or marked by childish misbehavior. Synonyms are mischievous, bad, and rude.

5. The correct answer id (D). Tidy means being clean and in good order.

6. The correct answer is (C). Matter-of-fact means adhering to the unembellished facts. Synonyms are plain, straightforward, or unemotional.

7. The correct answer is (B). In the last sentence of the story, Mrs. Darling expressed her disbelief to that Wendy said about Peter.

8. The correct answer is (A). The article talks not only about the rise in population thanks to better health-care but also the danger this growth poses on poorer countries when combined with climate change. It also debunks the myth that population is a problem but the way we consume.

9. The correct answer is (D). All the above are the dangers behind the population growth. In addition, with the way people consume resources and climate change, it will be more difficult for poorer countries where this trend is seen.

10. The correct answer is (A). This milestone was not unexpected. And it shows some good news: People are living longer, thanks in part to better healthcare.

11. The correct answer is (C). The trend will strain resources in these places. "The housing, roads, the hospitals, schools—everything is overstretched," says Gyang Dalyop, who works in urban planning in Nigeria.

12. The correct answer is (B). A milestone is a point in a chain of events at which an important change (as in one's fortunes) occurs. Synonyms are climax, landmark, and highlight.

13. The correct answer is (B). To overstretch means the act or an instance of stretching something beyond normal limits.

14. The correct answer is (A). Experts say the problem lies mainly with richer countries, like the United States and China. These countries consume the most energy and produce the most greenhouse-gas emissions.

15. The correct answer is (C). Scientists have found that floating solar panels could provide a huge amount of electricity if they were placed on lakes and other bodies of water around the world, which also help save water and protect land.

16. The correct answer is (A). But recently people have begun to explore putting floating solar panels on water. Because these panels float, some people call them "floatovoltaics."

17. The correct answer is (D). Floating solar panels could also help save water and protect land. They produce more than twice the amount of energy the United States generates in a year, and 10 times as much energy as all the solar power currently being generated in the world.

18. The correct answer is (B). Remarkable means worthy of being or likely to be noticed, especially as being uncommon or extraordinary.

19. The correct answer is (C). Drought means a period of dryness, especially when prolonged, specifically one that causes extensive damage to crop or prevents their successful growth.

20. The correct answer is (A). Floating solar panels could also help save water and protect land. They produce more than twice the amount of energy the United States generates in a year, and 10 times as much energy as all the solar power currently being generated in the world.

21. The correct answer is (B). After the researchers studied if 30% of 114,555 reservoirs worldwide will be covered by floating solar panels, they calculated that they generate more than twice the amount of energy the United States generates in a year and 10 times as much energy as all the solar power currently being generated in the world.

22. The correct answer is (A). If you happen to drop some cash by accident, Tokyo, Japan may be one of the best places to do it, because it is their law to turn in lost items including money. Tokyo police report that last year people turned in a record-breaking amount of lost money—roughly $29.6 million in cash.

23. The correct answer is (B). Tokyo police report that last year people turned in a record-breaking amount of lost money—roughly $29.6 million in cash, which is about $1.1 million more than the previous record, which was set in 2019.

24. The correct answer is (C). In Japan, people are expected to turn in any lost money that they find. It's actually a law and they have a reward system for people who turn in money they find.

25. The correct answer is (D). If someone claims money that has been turned in, the finder can get a reward worth up to 20% of the money and get the full amount after three months if no one claims it.

26. The correct answer is (D). They think it's because the coronavirus pandemic is ending; because the country changed its rules to allow more visitors and more people are going out.

27. The correct answer is (C). After three months, if no one has claimed the money, the finder gets to keep it all.

28. The correct answer is (B). Record-breaking means better, greater, higher, and so on, than any other in the past or beyond any previous record.

Section 4

Essay Writing

Stella was a peculiar little girl. She always says things other people don't understand. She talks about fairies, dwarves, and otherworldly creatures that most people believed were a product of her imagination, but Stella's father was always eager to listen to her. He was an explorer and had an aptitude for adventure. Her father often told her stories of his adventures in the forests.

One quiet afternoon, Stella was awakened from her nap. His father went to town and will be home later in the evening. She looked outside her window and saw a tail waving away into the forest. It was an unusual tail because it was the color of the rainbow. She immediately stood up and ran outside so she can catch up with the animal.

She followed the trail of footsteps the animal left and reached a meadow. There stood a horse-like creature with a single horn on its head and magnificent mane the color of the rainbow. She was astounded by what she saw but she didn't know what it was.

While she was admiring the sight of the animal, a man suddenly appeared from the bushes and whispered into her ears. He said, "Isn't it beautiful?" She turned around and saw her father smiling. "What is it, father?", she asked. "That's a unicorn, darling", her father answered.

SSAT Report

Scoring Methodology

On the **Middle and Upper Level SSAT**, a point is awarded for each correct answer, a quarter of a point is subtracted for each incorrect answer, and no points are awarded or deducted for omitted questions.

On the **Elementary Level SSAT**, a point is awarded for each correct answer and there is no penalty for incorrect answers.

Score Report Breakdown

Personal Information

The score report header details the student's basic information—name, address, date of birth, gender, etc. EMA will have scored the student at the grade displayed as indicated during registration. Please note that while gender is listed, SSAT scores are not gender-specific.

Total Score Summary

This section lists the two total scores.

"**Your score**" is the total scaled score, and the pointer indicates where the student's score is between the highest and lowest possible score. We also provide the average score for additional context.

The **total percentile** is on the right, comparing the student's scaled score to other SSAT test takers. This score shows the percentage of students that the student scored equal to or higher. For example, a 67th percentile indicates that the student scored equal to or higher than sixty-seven percent of test-takers in their grade.

Section Scores

In this section, EMA breaks score information into verbal, quantitative (math), and reading segments. Similar to the total score, a scaled score and percentile are shown, along with the average score. We also provide a score range; students who retest within a short period will likely score within this range. A breakdown explaining the main types of questions follows, including the number of questions answered correctly, incorrectly, and unanswered.

Here's a sample SSAT Report

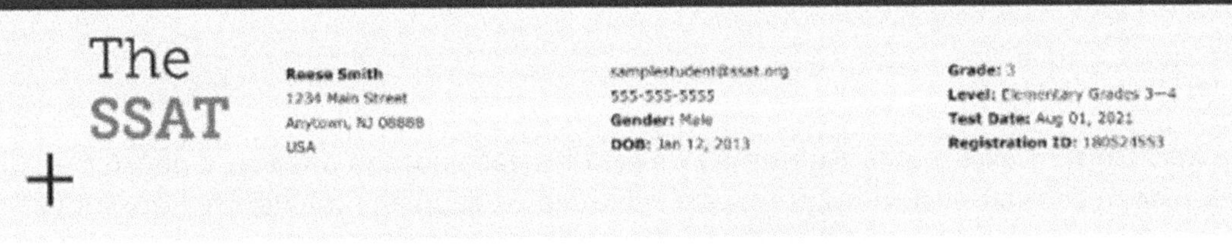

The SSAT

Reese Smith
1234 Main Street
Anytown, NJ 08888
USA

samplestudent@ssat.org
555-555-5555
Gender: Male
DOB: Jan 12, 2013

Grade: 3
Level: Elementary Grades 3–4
Test Date: Aug 01, 2021
Registration ID: 180524553

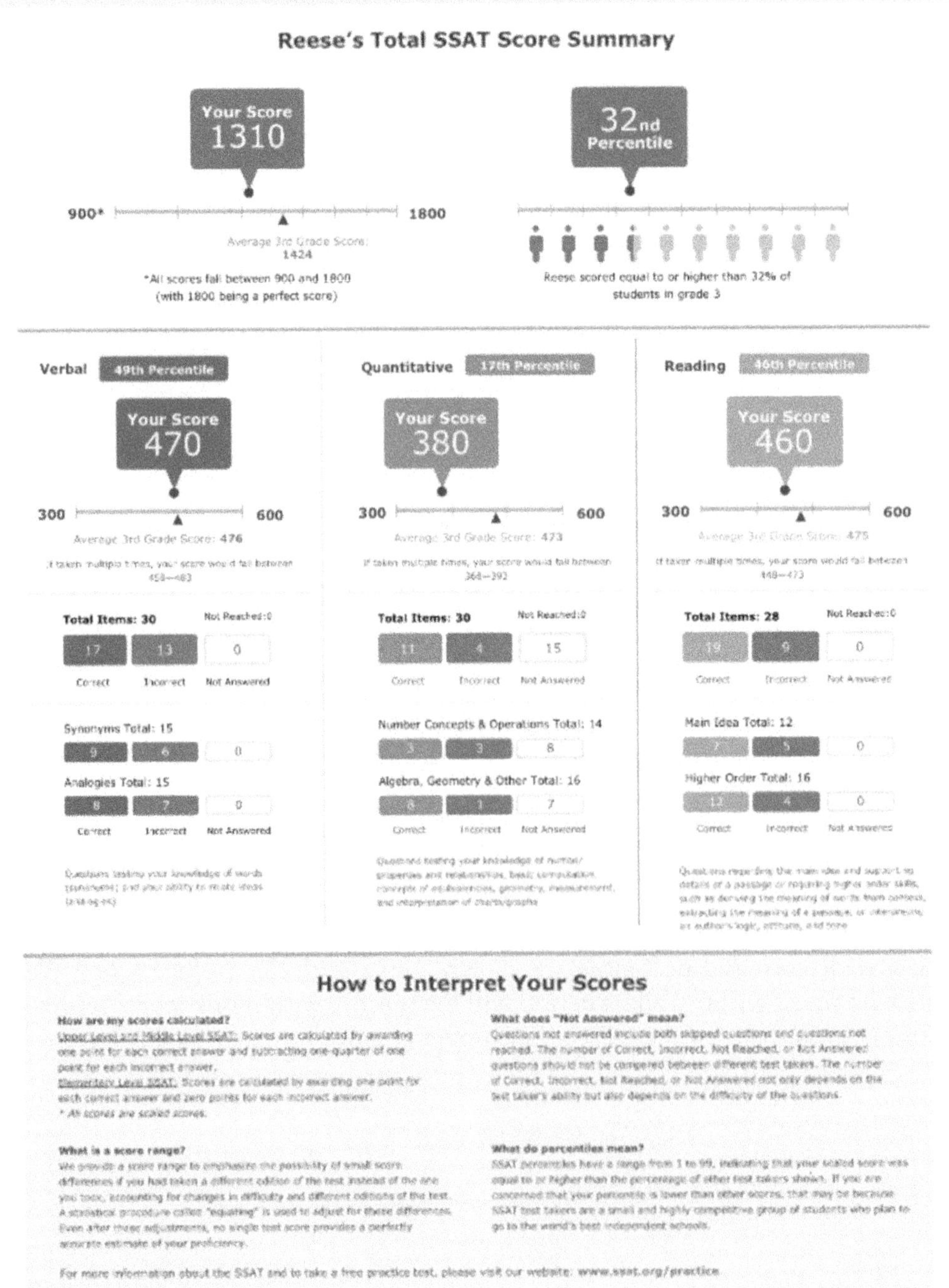

Reese's Total SSAT Score Summary

Your Score 1310

900* — 1800

Average 3rd Grade Score: 1424

*All scores fall between 900 and 1800 (with 1800 being a perfect score)

32nd Percentile

Reese scored equal to or higher than 32% of students in grade 3

Verbal 49th Percentile

Your Score 470

300 — 600

Average 3rd Grade Score: 476

If taken multiple times, your score would fall between 458—483

Total Items: 30 Not Reached:0

Correct	Incorrect	Not Answered
17	13	0

Synonyms Total: 15

Correct	Incorrect	Not Answered
9	6	0

Analogies Total: 15

Correct	Incorrect	Not Answered
8	7	0

Questions testing your knowledge of words (synonyms) and your ability to relate ideas (analogies)

Quantitative 17th Percentile

Your Score 380

300 — 600

Average 3rd Grade Score: 473

If taken multiple times, your score would fall between 368—392

Total Items: 30 Not Reached:0

Correct	Incorrect	Not Answered
11	4	15

Number Concepts & Operations Total: 14

Correct	Incorrect	Not Answered
3	3	8

Algebra, Geometry & Other Total: 16

Correct	Incorrect	Not Answered
8	1	7

Questions testing your knowledge of number properties and relationships, basic computation, concepts of equivalencies, geometry, measurement, and interpretation of charts/graphs

Reading 46th Percentile

Your Score 460

300 — 600

Average 3rd Grade Score: 475

If taken multiple times, your score would fall between 448—473

Total Items: 28 Not Reached:0

Correct	Incorrect	Not Answered
19	9	0

Main Idea Total: 12

Correct	Incorrect	Not Answered
7	5	0

Higher Order Total: 16

Correct	Incorrect	Not Answered
12	4	0

Questions regarding the main idea and supporting details of a passage or requiring higher order skills, such as deriving the meaning of words from context, extracting the meaning of a passage, or interpreting an author's logic, attitude, and tone

How to Interpret Your Scores

How are my scores calculated?
Upper Level and Middle Level SSAT: Scores are calculated by awarding one point for each correct answer and subtracting one-quarter of one point for each incorrect answer.
Elementary Level SSAT: Scores are calculated by awarding one point for each correct answer and zero points for each incorrect answer.
* All scores are scaled scores.

What is a score range?
We provide a score range to emphasize the possibility of small score differences if you had taken a different edition of the test instead of the one you took, accounting for changes in difficulty and different editions of the test. A statistical procedure called "equating" is used to adjust for these differences. Even after these adjustments, no single test score provides a perfectly accurate estimate of your proficiency.

What does "Not Answered" mean?
Questions not answered include both skipped questions and questions not reached. The number of Correct, Incorrect, Not Reached, or Not Answered questions should not be compared between different test takers. The number of Correct, Incorrect, Not Reached, or Not Answered not only depends on the test taker's ability but also depends on the difficulty of the questions.

What do percentiles mean?
SSAT percentiles have a range from 1 to 99, indicating that your scaled score was equal to or higher than the percentage of other test takers shown. If you are concerned that your percentile is lower than other scores, that may be because SSAT test takers are a small and highly competitive group of students who plan to go to the world's best independent schools.

For more information about the SSAT and to take a free practice test, please visit our website: www.ssat.org/practice

Registration ID: 180524553 | Reese Smith | 2020-2021 | SSAT Score Report

Page 1 of 1

Milton Keynes UK
Ingram Content Group UK Ltd.
UKHW052215190124
436359UK00004B/45